Love Story...
the real thing

Discovery Books

Love Story...
the real thing

by Bob Smith

WORD BOOKS, Publisher   **Waco, Texas**

First Printing, August 1975
Second Printing, July 1976

Scripture quotations, unless otherwise marked,
are from The Revised Standard Version of the Bible,
copyright 1946 (renewed 1973), 1956 and © 1971
by the Division of Christian Education of the
National Council of the Churches of Christ in
the United States of America, and are
used by permission.

Scripture quotations marked NAS are from The
New American Standard Bible © The Lockman
Foundation 1960, 1962, 1963, 1968, 1971.

Grateful acknowledgment is made for
AN AFFAIR TO REMEMBER
(OUR LOVE AFFAIR)
W: HAROLD ADAMSON, LEO MCCAREY
M: HARRY WARREN

COPYRIGHT © 1975 TWENTIETH CENTURY MUSIC CORPORATION
RIGHTS THROUGHOUT THE WORLD CONTROLLED BY LEO FEIST INC.
USED BY PERMISSION

ISBN 0-87680-989-1

Library of Congress catalog card number: 75–17111
Printed in the United States of America

LOVE STORY . . . THE REAL THING was prepared as
a staff research study at Peninsula Bible Church,
3505 Middlefield Road, Palo Alto, CA 94306

This book is dedicated
to the greatest Lover of all time,
"the One who loved us and gave Himself for us,"
Our Lord Jesus Christ

Contents

1.
Wanted: Happy Endings!

Where do I begin to tell the story of how great a love can be . . . ?

Perhaps we should start with this fact: *Our hearts are incurably romantic.* Somehow we have an instinctive sense of fitness which says there *should* be a happy ending to the story of every life and love. I've noticed this in the recent trend where the age of realism (telling it like it is in vivid, excruciating detail) is now becoming the age of nostalgia.

We respond with hurting hearts to the unfulfilled longings of a Romeo and Juliet, a Tristan and Isolde, and we feel that somehow there ought to be a change in the script.

You may recall a movie "An Affair to Remember," with Cary Grant and Deborah Kerr. It has replayed on television several times lately. Cary played the part of a love 'em and leave 'em playboy, and Deborah was mistress to a successful businessman. Neither of them knew anything about love though they were well acquainted with sex.

But they met and began to discover the deeper dimensions of real love. They found themselves beginning to care more for each other than they did for their own selfish interests, and they planned toward marriage. En route to the wedding, Deborah got in the way of a swerving car, and the resulting injury left her crippled. So she simply disappeared out of

Cary's life, leaving him waiting and wondering what had happened.

Here were two people in love who were, in effect, separated by love. Deborah was convinced that Cary should never see her again; she felt she couldn't inflict her crippled condition on the man she loved. The heartache and frustration of this situation builds to the climax of a Christmas Eve meeting of these two in which Cary, through his hurt and resentment, discovers her crippled condition. Their hearts are joined in the fulfillment of genuine love which is grounded in loving concern for each other instead of the shallowness of exploiting another sex partner.

And I must confess that I had as many tears in my eyes as they had in theirs at this point in the story. Here was a truly happy ending—the kind our hearts seem to expect. And I enjoy all over again the inner sense of gratification whenever I hear the theme melody:

> Our love affair is a wondrous thing,
> That we'll rejoice in remembering.
> Our love was born with our first embrace,
> And a page was torn out of time and space.
>
> Our love affair, may it always be
> a flame to burn through eternity.
> So, take my hand with a fervent prayer,
> That we may live and we may share
> a love affair to remember.

That's what we all want—a love affair to remember.

We need not settle for unhappy endings. There are definite reasons for our failure to achieve the fulfillment in life that we long for. There is a God who cares about us, who has good plans for us, if we will only seek to discover them. He's even written us his "Love Story"—for he's incurably romantic, too.

Will you explore with me how great a love can be—as we look for happy endings?

I Take Thee

The scene was one of beauty: beautiful bride, beautiful flowers, beautiful music, beautiful setting—and in this case two people expressing the reality of a beautiful relationship.

"Linda, it is the command of God, through his Word, that *a wife be subject to her husband* in everything, as the church is subject to Christ, for *the husband is the head of the wife,* as Christ is the head of the church.

"For you, this is to be the willing submission of love, based on your joint submission to each other, out of your mutual love for Christ. In these days of Women's Lib that is not a popular idea, but since you understand how the Lord loves you I trust you see that it is for your good— designed to give you the very fulfillment you desire. Besides, it's not a bad arrangement, for it gives your husband the ultimate responsibility for your marriage. The submission God commands is not painful or degrading, but ennobling, in that it reflects his concern to preserve order and harmony in appointing *one* to assume the responsibility of leadership in the family.

"And now, Linda, understanding and accepting this God-given order, do you take Don to be your husband, to join your lives together in living union, as Christ is to his church?"

"I do."

"Don, God commands in his Word, '*Husbands love your wives as Christ loved the church and gave himself for it.*'

"A man ought to give his wife the love he naturally has for his own body. The love a man gives his wife is the extending of his love for himself to enfold her. Nobody ever hates or neglects his own body; he feeds it and looks after it. And that is what Christ does for his body, the church. We who belong to Christ are members of that body, and thus enjoy all the benefits and blessings of his love.

"The leadership of love is the responsibility God gives to husbands, and it's no easy assignment. But what God requires of us, he also enables us to do. So, Don, understanding and accepting this responsibility, do you now take Linda to be your wife—to love her as Christ loves his Bride?"

"Yes, I do."

"Live your life together, then, with a due sense of responsibility, not as those who do not know the meaning and purpose of life, but as those who do. Make the best use of your time despite the difficulties of these days. Don't be vague, but firmly grasp what you know to be the will of the Lord. Don't get your stimulus from wine, but let the Spirit of God energize and control your lives. Express your joy in singing, with melody in your hearts, to the Lord. Thank God at all times for everything in the name of the Lord Jesus, and make allowances for each other out of reverence for Christ.

"And now, ministering in the name of Jesus Christ I pronounce you husband and wife."

Divergent Views

The bride and groom, facing their guests, were totally at ease—enjoying every moment, conscious of the significance of the occasion, showing at times sober faces, at times sparkling with glowing smiles. And once there was a hint of mistiness in their eyes. Theirs was the joy of entering into the beauty and glory of God's plan for marriage.

But how about their guests? How did they understand this scene?

A bridesmaid who signed the license as a witness expressed her view: "Wow, I'd never say the vows that Linda spoke! What's all that submission bit? Didn't she ever hear of Women's Lib?"

And the policeman regulating parking expressed himself clearly: "I've heard lots of wedding ceremonies, but that one really got to me! I used to go to church, and I think I'd better round up my family next Sunday and get back in it. Know of a good church?"

A young couple put it this way: "It was so good to hear the Lord included in this marriage. We didn't understand it that way when we were married. Makes us want to get married again—this time with the Lord in the picture."

Another man, a single fellow, said, "I'm *never* going to get married! What that guy said scared me right out of the wedding scene."

And another, this time a young woman: "Why should I tie myself to one man in that kind of slavery when I can play the field and have 'em all?"

What's It All About?

These are samples of actual comments from people at weddings, displaying a wide divergence of views about marriage. How come? Why does it look so good to some and so absolutely abhorrent to others?

Possibly there are as many answers to that as there are people, but I'd like to suggest a few general observations.

First, there are people who have seen too many bad marriages to think that any marriage can be good. With the high divorce rate, the proportion of children from broken homes is high. These children acquire a mighty dim view of marriage. Many others see nothing but bitterness and bickering in homes which are not yet broken, but are badly fractured.

Then there is the impact of the permissive society in which we live, with the convenience of the "pill" and the ready availability of free love—"sex on the street corner."

Perhaps most devastating—many young men growing up have never seen a real man as God intended man to be, and thus have not seen authentic love—God's love—demonstrated in real life by their parents. Cop-out fathers and overly protective, dominant mothers hardly paint an attractive picture of wedded bliss!

Whatever the reasons, the prevalence of a low view of marriage is unmistakable and undeniable.

But what about those who have a high view of marriage? How did they get that way? Where do they get their information?

May I suggest that somehow they have caught a glimpse of the REAL THING—the way God intended it to be? And if there is anything the world needs these days it is to recapture something of the beauty of God's plan in marriage! The dissolution of the family in modern society, I submit, is the most devastating problem we face. With this in mind, would you seek to understand with me the true "LOVE STORY—THE REAL THING?"

Hearing from the Author

In order to do this, we must listen once again to the author of marriage, the one who originated the idea—God himself.

God is very fond of the idea of marriage. He must be, because his Word is full of it. Early in Genesis God presented Eve to Adam in the first marriage (Gen. 2:18–25) and laid down the foundational guidelines for the relationship. At the end of the Bible, in Revelation, we see "the marriage supper of the Lamb" (Rev. 19:9) and the introduction of "the Bride, the wife of the Lamb" (Rev. 21:9). So we have the entire Word of God bracketed with the idea of marriage. And between Genesis and Revelation what do we find? Israel is called *the wife of Jehovah* in the Old Testament (Ezek. 16:32), and the church is pictured as *the Bride of Christ* in the New Testament (2 Cor. 11:2). It would seem that God rates marriage as a very important and highly valued relationship.

Perhaps the most exalted presentation (and I find the least understood) is in Ephesians 5, where the relationship of husband and wife is paralleled with that of Christ and his church. In marital and pre-marital counseling I am constantly amazed at how little we understand of all that God tells us in such a concise package. Often it is a case of "When all else fails, read the directions." And when we do, we find the Designer unrolls the blueprint of his design for Christian marriage.

2.

God's "Elevation View" of Marriage

If we were to call Genesis 2:18–25 "God's Plan View of Marriage" because it shows the general layout, like the top view in an architectural drawing, then we could call Ephesians 5:21–33 the "Elevation View"—the view from the ground up, because it presents a very elevated or highly exalted view of the marriage relationship.

The key to our understanding of this Ephesians passage is careful observation to give us clear understanding of marriage from God's perspective. Let's examine the text:

FOR BOTH: Be subject to one another out of reverence for Christ.

FOR WIVES: Wives, be subject to your husbands, as to the Lord. For the husband is the head of the wife as Christ is the head of the church, his body, and is himself its Savior. As the church is subject to Christ, so let wives also be subject in everything to their husbands.

FOR HUSBANDS: Husbands, love your wives, as Christ loved the church and gave himself up for

her, that he might sanctify her, having
cleansed her by the washing of water with
the word, that he might present the
church to himself in splendor, without
spot or wrinkle or any such thing, that
she might be holy and without blemish.
Even so husbands should love their wives
as their own bodies. He who loves his
wife loves himself. For no man ever hates
his own flesh, but nourishes and cherishes
it, as Christ does the church, because we
are members of his body. "For this reason a man shall leave his father and
mother and be joined to his wife, and the
two shall become one."

FOR BOTH:　　　This is a great mystery, and I take it to
mean Christ and the church; however, let
each one of you love his wife as himself,
and let the wife see that she respects her
husband (Eph. 5:21–33).

The first thing we need to observe is the form of expression used in the passage. It is not hard to see that it is a comparison, or analogy. We catch this in the repeated use of "as"
and "so." This and other clues throughout the passage indi-
cate we are to consider a side-by-side comparison. With this
in mind, let's look carefully at the details.

Mutual Subjection?

"Be subject to one another out of reverence for Christ"
(Eph. 5:21). This is the umbrella verse which covers all the
human relationships mentioned in this particular passage

and extending into Chapter 6. Being subject to one another out of reverence for Christ is the governing principle for husbands and wives, children and fathers, slaves and masters. But what is this mutual subjection which God commands? The term in the Greek text means "to rank under." But how can everyone rank under everyone else? If someone takes the lower rank, wouldn't someone else have to be on top? It would seem contradictory, but it really is not; it is dealing with our attitude toward others and simply means that we should take the second place in favor of the other person.

> Let each of you look not only to his own interests, but also to the interests of others. Have this mind among yourselves, which you have in Christ Jesus (Phil. 2:4–5).

The Christian mind-set is to be the same as we see in Christ! This is a pretty good start—to get our attitude straight.

But what is our Lord's attitude?

> . . . who, though he was in the form of God, did not count equality with God a thing to be grasped, but emptied himself, taking the form of a servant, being born in the likeness of men. And being found in human form he humbled himself and became obedient unto death, even death on a cross (Phil. 2:6–8).

It is not hard to see how beautifully this important principle would work—if only we would fulfill it. Then there's . . .

A Word to the Wives

> Wives, be subject to your husbands, as to the Lord. For the husband is the head of the wife as Christ is the head of

the church, his body, and is himself its Savior. As the church is subject to Christ, so let wives also be subject in everything to their husbands (Eph. 5:22–24).

Here we have God's word to wives, beginning with a command, "Wives, be subject to your husbands." Now, this is a hard line for many women. They envision everything from chauvinism to slavery, and certainly second-class citizenship, if nothing else. But I know many women who are completely at ease with this idea, some (including my wife) who welcome it! And I find that usually those who object to it don't really understand the concept as God intended it should be viewed.

One day a lady phoned me with the question, "How can I submit to a husband I can't even respect?" At first it seemed to be an unanswerable question, but as I opened my Bible to this passage (not a bad practice, I find—to check the context), the answer leaped out at me: ". . . as to the Lord." So I proceeded to explain that the performance of her husband, whether good or bad, was not involved here—*only her obedience to the Lord.*

If we read on, it says, "For the husband is the head of the wife as Christ is the head of the church." The little word "for" introduces the explanation. It is saying, "Be submissive simply because I have set things up this way: the man is to be the head." It's out of reverence for Christ and in obedience to his demands, which come from his loving concern for us, that we find it possible to respond.

True Submission

Is submission just "lying down and playing dead"?

Do I become just a doormat for my husband? Is it to be a master-slave relationship?

Certainly not. And if you think any of these ideas even

remotely reflect the truth, you need to think again! There
are biblical statements which resolve each of these questions.

First, there are no second-class citizens in the kingdom of
God. In Christ, "There is neither Jew nor Greek, there is
neither slave nor free, there is no male or female; for you
are all one in Christ Jesus" (Gal. 3:28). All distinctions cease
in our relationships before the Lord. All are equal in his
eyes. He holds all of us in equally high value! Secondly, how
can a "door-mat" be a helper? You may recall that the number one assignment to the woman in Genesis 2:18 is to be
". . . a helper fit for him."

I appreciate how my wife, Pearl, fulfills her assignment. She
will say to me on occasion, "Now, dear, promise you won't
get mad at me if I tell you something." I laugh a bit self-
consciously, knowing I've got something coming, and say,
"Okay, give it to me." Then she will point out some area
of needed correction to help me shape up. And if my male
ego rears its ugly head and I start building defenses, she
simply pulls this punch line on me: "Now, honey, please
listen to me because God made me your helper. But I can't
help if you won't let me!" And she has me dead to rights!
She would not be fulfilling her God-given assignment if she
just played the "door-mat" or settled for "gag rule."

"Well," you say, "this sounds more like equality. Where's
the submission line?"

Submission always has a headship in view. And headship
involves final responsibility in making decisions. Let me
illustrate:

1 Corinthians 11:3 tells us, ". . . I want you to understand
that the head of every man is Christ, the head of the woman
is her husband, and the head of Christ is God." This is a
very revealing statement, perhaps the key verse in helping us
understand headship.

The most startling fact is that ". . . the head of Christ is

God." This says that even in the Godhead there is headship. I don't know how you view the Trinity, but I find it helpful to use an illustration from my former business life, keeping in mind that any analogy always falls short of the reality by the very nature of the case. In any corporation there are officers: Chairman of the Board, Vice President, etc. So I liken God the Father to Chairman of the Board. He stays in the home office and runs the company. The Son is the Executive Vice President, and as frequently happens, he is sent out of the office to do a job—in this case he went out to accomplish a redemptive mission and then returned to headquarters. The Holy Spirit is the Sales Manager of the corporation, since he comes to us to present the work of the Son (John 16:13–15). All three are equally members of "the Firm," yet each has a different function in representing the corporation. But ONLY ONE is the head! "The head of Christ is God."

If you want to look further at this idea, read 1 Corinthians 15:24–28 which declares the subjection of the Son to God the Father. (Remember, though, that each member of the Godhead [the Firm] shares in an equality of being and nature.)

So, God's Word sets before you wives a living example in your submission assignment—the Son of God himself! As one of my fellow pastors points out, in both the Godhead and in marriage relationships there are three areas to consider—like this:

	The Godhead	Husband and Wife
In their PERSON	EQUALITY	EQUALITY
In their WORK	DIVERSITY	DIVERSITY
In final RESPONSIBILITY	ONE HEAD—GOD	ONE HEAD—the HUSBAND

This allocation of responsibility is not only possible, but necessary, to preserve order and harmony in marriage. It allows the husband to be responsible to ONE LORD!

No Two-Headed Monster!

One other comment about 1 Corinthians 11:3: ". . . the head of every man is Christ." This is an unalterable fact, and the submission of the wife is designed to free the man to relate to ONE head—not to a two-headed monstrosity. If the wife tries to run her husband instead of letting Christ be his head, she faces him with an impossibility, for as our Lord said, "No man can serve two masters; for either he will hate the one and love the other, or he will be devoted to one and despise the other" (Matt. 6:24). Do you wives want your husbands to love you and be devoted to you? Then give them the freedom to respond to one Lord! Not that your basic motivation should be self-centered, for we are to obey "as unto the Lord," but there is a legitimate area of self-interest in which the Lord wants us to enjoy the fulfillment resulting from the obedience of faith.

Real Women's Liberation

Real freedom for a wife is to trust the Lord to handle her husband! It isn't because men are so wise and wonderful that wives are asked to submit; it's because the Lord Jesus is wise and wonderful—and fully capable of handling even a rebellious mate!

As usual, the beauty and value of God's way shines through: Walking according to his way we're not stuck with the frailties of man, we're tied into the adequacy of our Lord.

"Wives, be subject to your husbands, as to the Lord" (Eph. 5:22). Wonderful words—"AS TO THE LORD."

In Everything?

You mean in everything? That's what it says. The only possible exception (implicit because of teaching elsewhere in Scripture, as in Acts 4:19–20) is the case in which a husband asks his Christian wife to do something clearly prohibited by God in his Word. For instance, if a non-Christian husband should ask his Christian wife to engage in a wife-swapping arrangement, she must obey God rather than her husband. The Lordship of Christ has prior claim in any such situation. The first and great commandment, Jesus said, is to "love the Lord, your God"—then the second, "Love your neighbor."

In every other situation a wife is to be submissive to her husband. She has the "follower," not the "leader" assignment. She is to be his helper. That means she is to cooperate in fulfilling *his* goals and plans.

You mean even when he is wrong? Yes, even when he is wrong! One of the greatest ways we learn is through our mistakes. And the Lord doesn't tell us we'll never make a mistake, does he? Submission means giving him the liberty to fail, as well as to succeed—to be wrong as well as to be right.

My dear wife knows she has not only the *right,* but the *responsibility* to disagree with me when it's necessary. This is the way it often works with us: There will be a matter of importance to both of us, so I'll say, "Let's talk about this matter, dear. Here's the way I see it." And I'll proceed to outline the course of action I think is right. But she may not agree, so she says, "I think you've got it all wrong, and here's why." So she tells me what she thinks about the matter. We discuss it fully, reviewing all the issues, and finally I may say, "I appreciate going over the situation with you, but I am still not persuaded. I'm going ahead the way I outlined." So she replies, "I still think you're wrong, but right or wrong I'm with you. It's your responsibility to decide."

That is real submission! And the check-out comes if, in those instances when I prove to be wrong, she *doesn't* say "I told you so!"

That's *real* submission because it means she's trusting the Lord—even for my mistakes.

3.
And Now-for the Husbands

For some reason, the Lord has more to say to husbands than to wives in the Ephesians passage. Perhaps it's because of the weighty responsibility of the man's headship—or it could be because we men are so slow to catch on and so reluctant to obey God's good word to us. Whatever the reason, let's open the door to a personal understanding of God's blueprint for a happy home in his word to husbands. It's personal spiritual suicide not to!

Husbands, love your wives as Christ loved the church and gave himself up for her . . . (Eph. 5:25).

It's interesting to note that God never commands wives to love their husbands (even though in Titus 2:4 it is clear they *are* to love them), but his first word to husbands is a command to love their wives. It seems that for a woman to give love is easier and more natural than for a man. Their heart commitment, it appears to me, comes rather easily from their God-given sensitivity. Theirs is a whole-hearted response and steadfast allegiance which seems to flow naturally from the quality of life they possess. I'm speaking here primarily about Christian women, but I see the same readiness of response also in the fact that it seems easier for women to come to Christ than for men. We men are often such proud, hard-headed, hard-hearted characters. And when it comes to receiving and expressing love, we're such clumsy clods!

So God says "Husbands, love your wives." It's the very word we need, just as wives need the command, "Be subject to your husbands."

Love Commanded!

But how do you command love? Is it possible to produce love on demand? Isn't love an emotional response? And how do you produce an emotional response on demand?

The answers to all these queries revolve around the way we define "love." And, I submit, here's a subject worth thinking about! Everyone's talking about love; everyone needs it. Most of the popular songs we hear and sing focus on it, but almost nobody knows what it is! A popular television interviewer often poses this question to his guest stars, and I've noticed that most of them stumble all over themselves trying to answer and usually come up with some inept and inadequate reply.

How do you define it?

I must confess I laid a trap for you in suggesting that love is an emotional response, because it is not! At least, emotion is not the primary ingredient—even though it may be, and usually is—involved. Let me give you the definition of love that I've found satisfactory:

Love is a commitment of the will to do that which will benefit the loved one—even at great personal cost, and even when there is no response of love.

Where do I get this definition? It's not hard to discover. All we need to do is look at Jesus Christ. Scripture tells us that he "loved me and gave himself for me" (Gal. 2:20*b*), and as I review what this means in terms of life actions, I have a mental picture of Jesus from Gethsemane to the Cross.

Our Lord's prayer in the garden is very revealing: "My Father, if it be possible let this cup pass from me; nevertheless, not as I will, but as thou wilt" (Matt. 26:39*b*). As I see this, our Lord is saying in modern parlance, "Father, I don't really like the way I'm heading; the prospect of the cross is abhorrent to me—to be 'made sin' is a horrible way to go. If there's any other way, let's take it."

I'm certain that none of us can even remotely sense the awful revulsion our Lord felt at the prospect of becoming the "garbage dump" for all the vileness of the human race. It's as if all the rottenness of every heinous and repulsive sin of the whole race of mankind were placed in one pile on the sinless Son of God.

Again, I say, we who have learned so well to accommodate sin in our lives can hardly grasp what this would be like for One who did no sin, who knew no sin, and in whom is no sin (1 Peter 2:22; 2 Cor. 5:21; 1 John 3:5).

Yet Jesus said, ". . . not as I will, but as you will." Note that our Lord had a will to exercise, but he chose to coincide with the will of his Father! The old argument as to whether or not Christ could have sinned pales into insignificance here. The fact is that he willfully *chose* to go the appointed route to the cross. He loved us and gave himself for us. The "loving" was the "giving," as he deliberately chose that which shriveled his soul because he knew we needed a Savior.

So, I say, if we take our Lord's exposition of love, we see that it is volition, not emotion, which is the chief factor. Emotion can follow, but if we limit our understanding of love to be a "warm feeling" (as so many understand it), we miss its main thrust and import. Certainly our Lord had no warm feeling when he thought of the cross. And it's equally un-

likely he had any warm feeling when he thought about us—
helpless, ungodly, sinners, and hostile to God as we were
(see Rom. 5:6–10). It was only the *result* of his willing
sacrifice of himself that held any pleasant prospect, so that
". . . for the joy that was set before him he endured the
cross, despising the shame" (Heb. 12:2*b*). There followed
as the result of his commitment of love the joy of doing the
Father's will and of welcoming many sons to glory. So it is to
be with husbands in the love relationship of marriage. Love
is a commitment of the will—so God can *command* us to
love our wives. As we obey, then we can enjoy the warm
feeling of a satisfying and fulfilling love relationship, but
obedience comes first.

As Christ Loved?

But how in the world can I love as Christ loved? I don't
naturally love that way. His is love which never "turns off,"
but mine turns off at the slightest rebuff or inconvenience.
The answer is not far away: only Christ loves as Christ loves,
and this love can only come from him as a source. So husbands are to be stretched out on him by faith—the full
weight of our confidence and expectation is to be on him.
After all, that's why he came to live in us when we invited
him to be our Lord. This is the love which is "flooded into
our hearts by the Holy Spirit who is given to us" (Rom. 5:5,
Phillips). There's no love shortage if we just draw on the
available resources we enjoy in Christ through the Spirit of
Christ who indwells us. By choice we choose to obey—then
his love flows.

The Christian's Power Source

The backdrop of God's words both to husbands and wives

is the instruction of Ephesians 5:18 ". . . be filled with the Spirit," which means continually being *controlled* and *empowered* by the Holy Spirit, the enabling Person of the Godhead who indwells every believer in Christ. He is the one who will supply all the love we need as long as we recognize that this kind of love is not home-made or pumped up from our own unaided human effort and determination. This love is the product of his life in us.

"Husbands, love your wives, as Christ loved the church and gave himself up for her." We have, in this, a command to do what is naturally impossible for us, but supernaturally, it is not only possible, but reasonable, normal, and necessary. It's helpful to remember at this point that God never demands of us more than he will himself supply, as we trust him.

"As Christ loves" carries with it another feature: It is not dependent on the response or behavior of the loved one. I've found I need the love of Christ most when I'm misbehaving the worst. And he always gets to me, because instead of withdrawing his love, he patiently and lovingly persists in showing me he still loves me. Even so should husbands love their wives!

Love with a Purpose

The next two verses, Ephesians 5:25–27, express the very heart of God's purpose in marriage and are especially directed to the attention of husbands. Husbands, love . . . as Christ loved . . . for a purpose. And the Apostle proceeds to spell out that purpose:

> . . . *that* he might sanctify her, having cleansed her by the washing of water with the word, *that* he might present the church to himself in splendor, without spot or wrinkle

or any such thing, *that* she might be holy and without blemish (Eph. 5:26–27).

Remember, at this point, the comparison the writer has in mind is like this:

AS with CHRIST and the CHURCH	SO with HUSBANDS and WIVES
CHRIST LOVED for a purpose	HUSBANDS are to LOVE for a purpose

With this as a heading, let's fill out the details of the analogy in order to discover the three-fold purpose toward which Christ loved and the corresponding features in the husband-wife relationship.

First, Christ loved us "that he might sanctify" us. What do you suppose that means? The word "sanctify" is one of those "holy" words we often use without clear understanding and definition. My fellow pastor, Ray Stedman, uses the best definition of this term I have encountered: to sanctify is "to put to the intended use," that is, to devote something to that designed end for which it was made. To sanctify a pen, we write with it; to sanctify a chair, we sit on it, etc. How, then, does Christ "sanctify" a person? Obviously he puts us to the use for which he intended us. But what is that?

This question has far-reaching implications which we won't pretend to exhaust, but the first thing which comes to my mind is that we were made in the image of God—to reflect his person and character. We were made for "godlikeness" or "godliness." To use a modern illustration, we are to be "transceivers"—like radios which receive and transmit—to receive and transmit a consistent message which portrays

God's character among men who need to see what God is like.

This idea is clearly portrayed in 2 Corinthians 3:18 ". . . we all, with unveiled face, beholding [literally, "mirroring"—beholding and reflecting] the glory of the Lord, are being changed into his likeness from one degree of glory to another." And later in the same passage: "For it is . . . God who said, 'let light shine out of darkness,' who has shone in our hearts to give the light [or, the "shining forth"] of the knowledge of the glory of God in the face of Christ" (2 Cor. 4:6).

As a Christian, I learn from this that Christ loved me and gave himself for me in order that he might give me a sense of purpose which dignifies my existence—to be the common earthenware vessel which holds a great treasure, the risen Lord himself (2 Cor. 4:7). This is something of what it means to be "sanctified" by the love of Christ. And we could go from there to the fact that the Lord has given a ministry to every one of his own and spiritual gifts to fulfill his good purposes in that significant function. No doubt you can think of many more ways he sanctifies us.

Now, the Other Side

So much for the "Christ and the Church" side of the analogy. Now how about the other side, the "husband and wife" side? What does it mean for a husband to sanctify his wife? Toward what purpose are we to love our wives?

If we think back to the beginning of marriage, we remember that the Lord God said, "It is not good for man to be alone; I will make him a helper fit for him" (Gen. 2:18). So we reflect that God's purpose in giving Adam a wife was to complement him and fulfill his life. A *shared life* is his first aim. How, then, do I sanctify my wife?—by sharing my life with her in every way and not shutting her out. I must let her be who she is *by God's appointment*, my helper. And certainly there's no way she can help me if I don't count her in on all the action. I've learned by personal experience and in much marital counseling that the most devastating thing we can do to our wives is to give them the impression that we're shutting them out of our lives.

God put it this way: "To the woman he said, '. . . your desire shall be for your husband'" (Gen. 3:16*b*). A man's life-interests are of necessity divided, but a woman's heart is centered in her man. No wonder so many wives have such a hard time; we men violate the essential features of the marriage relationship so easily, without even trying. But in reality, husbands are to be transparent before their wives, clearly and openly sharing their lives with them so they find it easy to fulfill their God-given "helper" responsibility.

In what other ways does a husband "sanctify" his wife? One way, which is quite often neglected, is to recognize and remember that she is a *person* as well as a wife. She is a unique, one-of-a-kind, original from the hand of God, with her own personality, gifts, talents, and ministry. I know husbands who keep their wives on a leash, like they would a dog—they can't go out or engage in any activity outside the home without special permission from the "king." I know one Christian man who won't even let his wife go to a Bible class or go shopping without his permission. No wonder Women's Lib was born! A husband should not only *allow*, but actively *encourage* his wife to express her own personality and being as a woman. She wasn't made *just* to be his wife; she is also to be a unique expression of the life of the Christ who indwells her, for in Christ "there is neither male nor female; for you are all one in Christ Jesus" (Gal. 3:28).

Also, women have been given gifts by the Holy Spirit which are just as necessary to the well-being of the Body of Christ as are the men's. If they aren't encouraged to discover and employ their gifts, then the whole Body will be hurting to the degree they fail to do so.

Then There's "Oikodespotes"

An almost totally ignored concept is expressed in these words: "I will, therefore, that the younger women marry, bear children, *guide the house,* give no occasion to the adversary to speak reproachfully" (1 Tim. 5:14 A.V.). The word in the Greek text translated "guide the house" is a compound word, *oikos,* which means "house" or "home," and *despotes,* which is usually translated "lord" or "master." We get our English word "despot" from it. A wife is to be the *ruler of the home* according to this Scripture. This means that the home is to be the wife's domain, the place where she is to reign. Our modern equivalent of this word would be "homemaker."

Our American scene suffers from an obvious lack of homemakers. On the one hand we see cop-out husbands who fail to exercise leadership of any kind, let alone spiritual leadership, and on the other hand there are career-women wives who are not making homes for their families. And the result is that there are lots of houses but very few homes and a generation of freaked-out young people who prefer hippie communes to what they've seen of "home." The greatest career to which women could aspire, in God's book, is to be the "ruler" at home as God intended, especially when we consider that as a mother, she has the greatest influence on the lives of the children in those important early formative years.

How can a husband sanctify his wife? Let her be the homemaker. If *she* doesn't make the home it won't be made. Have you ever seen a bachelor pad? It usually bears little resemblance to a home. But what could be more valuable than the warm place of shelter and love that home represents? Home is to be a haven—a place of security and acceptance —where we can be known and loved exactly as we are. Both the headship of the husband and the homemaking of the wife are needed to fulfill the beauty of God's plan for the home. I well remember how, in my ignorance of these principles, I violated God's order expressed in them. I bought a house without my wife's having seen it! When we drove up to view it, instead of jumping for joy as I expected her to do, she burst into tears. As I look back, I think about myself, "How dumb can you get!"

Back to the Analogy

The second expression of purpose is: ". . . that he might present the church to himself in splendor, without spot or wrinkle or any such thing" (Eph. 5:27*a*). If we follow through both sides of the analogy again we discover:

CHRIST LOVED US	HUSBANDS, LOVE YOUR WIVES
That (1) he might present us to himself in splendor. (2) the church might be brought to perfection and fulfillment.	That (1) your wife may be a joy to your own heart and life. (2) she may be brought to the fulfillment of her womanhood through your leadership of love.

The first thing we observe here is that Christ loved unselfishly, but as a result, he reaped a dividend that he could enjoy. I love this idea that the Lord Jesus is going to enjoy the benefits of his self-giving love. The One who has everything somehow gains something it seems he always wanted —a perfect, holy, and chaste Bride, without flaw. This is a fulfillment of an earlier statement in Ephesians: ". . . and he [God, the Father] put all things under his [Christ's] feet and has made him head over all things for the church, which is his body, *the fulness of him who fills all in all*" (Eph. 1:22–23). Here's a paradox: The One who fills everything has something added to his fullness—in the church. What an amazing truth—that we can contribute something to the Lord's fullness! My personal desire is to be a strongly contributing party to this kind of action.

The other point here is: The loving purpose of our Lord is to bring us to the fulfillment of our humanity. As unlikely as it may seem, he is going to present us faultless to himself! (See Jude 24) He is going to conform each of us to his own image (Rom. 8:29). You may look at yourself, or me, and say, "I don't see how he can do it," but Jesus declares that this is the very purpose toward which his love is directed! What does this mean to husbands on the other side of the analogy? I see two startling parallels: (1) The action of a husband toward his wife is reflexive; that is, it reverts back on him; and (2) the husband is responsible for the fulfillment of his wife both as a woman and as a wife. It's part of his headship responsibility.

"Hey," you say, "that's heavy!" And I agree. I've asked the Lord, "Are you sure I signed up for this course?" And he assures me that I did and that my response to the challenge (and to his sufficiency) is a checkout on my Christian manhood! This, if nothing else, is enough to face me with the constant necessity of trusting him to produce in me all that he demands, as I walk by faith in him.

There's one more expression of God's purpose in the passage we're considering: ". . . that she might be holy and without blemish" (Eph. 5:27*b*). This one seems to be quite closely linked with the previous one, as indeed all three expressions of purpose are closely tied and interrelated. But I think it adds one more basic thought—that of a finality of commitment to see it through to completion, like this:

CHRIST LOVED US	HUSBANDS, LOVE YOUR WIVES
Toward the end that our devotion to him will be total: he intends to bring us through to perfection, to being wholly his.	To the consummation of the ultimate fulfillment of your love relationship—a permanent commitment on your part to finish the job.

For husbands this says there's no escape clause in our marriage contract—no back door out of the arrangement. By contrast with the "easy in, easy out" arrangements the world makes, this lays it on the line. The casual, worldly view of marriage is like playing musical chairs: When the music stops we change partners, but not without all the misery and pain that broken love relationships bring! Because the marriage relationship is designed by God to be so great, it is the deepest kind of hurt when it doesn't work out the way he intends.

Communication

You may have noticed that I skipped over one clause. I did it purposely so we could consider it separately. It's the modifying clause, ". . . having cleansed her by the washing of water with the word" (Eph. 5:26). There's some very important information in this as we follow through the analogy.

As for Christ and the church, we recall our Lord's words to his own: ". . . you are already made clean through the word which I have spoken to you" (John 15:3). The word of the gospel is that cleansing word which initially fit us for fellowship with a holy God and then continues to keep us cleaned up as we walk with him. John adds further teaching on this matter in his first letter:

> If we say we have fellowship with him while we walk in darkness, we lie and do not live according to the truth; but if we walk in the light, as he is in the light, we have fellowship with one another, and the blood of Jesus his Son cleanses [literally, "keeps on cleansing"] us from all sin. If we confess our sins, he is faithful and just and will forgive our sins and cleanse us from all unrighteousness" (1 John 1:6–7, 9).

Cleansing through communication is what this spells out. We have a love relationship with our Lord, and love communicates—to keep things open and honest—so that we can enjoy the relationship. Confession of sin is just keeping things open and honest before our Lord.

So it is for husbands and wives. Our love relationship can be kept fresh and sweet and enjoyable only so long as we keep it clean through communication. Our Lord is saying to husbands, "Talk to your wife!" Psychologists point out that failure to communicate is the most common cause of marital problems. But the Word of God said it centuries ago before psychologists were ever heard of!

And notice who is to initiate the communication! In our Lord's case, he did; he initiated the costly communication of the Word of God, the Incarnation, and the Cross. His love demanded that he open up his heart to us in unmistakable terms to share his own thoughts and character with us. So, husbands, it seems apparent that we can do no less. According to my experience, this is the hardest thing we have to do. I come home to my wife after a full day of talking and listening (since the business of a pastor is essentially that of communicating) and my wife wants to share in my day. It's my job to initiate communication between us. And it's hard. But the Lord keeps reminding me, "Who ever said it would be easy? Remember what it cost me to get the message across to you, and how I still have trouble getting you to listen?" So I get the message that I'm to do it anyway.

My wife has a helpful way of encouraging communication. She asks, "Got any news?" There's an eager look on her face and I get the point. She is really saying, "Talk to me. I'm interested in everything that happens to you. You're important to me! Am I important to you? I want to share your life!" So I communicate—sometimes only enough to tell her, "Honey, I'm sure there's lots I can tell you, but I'm too tired right now. How about tomorrow morning over a cup of coffee?" And that's all it takes to assure her that I'm not ignoring her, that I care. Then I need to be sure to initiate the conversation in the morning.

Then, there's the matter of reestablishing communication which has been broken. And, returning to the analogy: the husband is responsible to initiate reconciliation, even as Christ moved to reconcile man to God. This gets especially tough when the husband happens to be right and his wife is wrong in the issue over which they have disagreed. It takes the same kind of caring communication that Christ initiated toward us.

4.

Getting It All Together

It may be helpful to summarize our findings so far in chart form:

AS with CHRIST AND THE CHURCH CHRIST LOVED US and gave HIMSELF for us . . .	SO with HUSBANDS AND WIVES HUSBANDS, LOVE your WIVES as CHRIST LOVED the CHURCH . . .
THAT we might be put to the intended use for which he created us: (a) as an expression of his own LIFE and CHARACTER. (b) to fulfill our calling, enjoy our God-given ministries. (c) exercise our spiritual gifts —and much more (you add the rest).	THAT she might SHARE YOUR LIFE, be your helper, etc.: (a) expressing her own personality and life in CHRIST. (b) employing her gifts in a spiritual ministry. (c) be the RULER of the HOME, in all that means to you and your children.
THAT he might enjoy the benefits stemming from his unselfish love—in enjoying his Bride. And lead us on to the fulfillment of our manhood and womanhood by his love.	THAT you may enjoy the beauty and glory of her fulfilled womanhood, as you undertake the responsibility of your headship—leading her with the leadership of love to ultimate fulfillment.

THAT his work in us may go on to completion, that we may be wholly his.	THAT your commitment may may be steadfast and permanent, in spite of problems.
Based on COMMUNICATION which his loving heart initiates —to keep us close, mutually enjoying our love relationship.	Remembering that LOVE finds a way to COMMUNICATE, and it's your initiative if you are going to love as CHRIST LOVED.

Notice, in all we've considered about the responsibilities of husbands and wives there is *no mutual contingency clause.* The Lord says, "Wives, submit . . ." and "Husbands, love . . ."; he doesn't say, "Wives, submit yourselves to your husbands as long as they are loving you as I love you"—or "Husbands, love your wives, as long as they submit to you." This rules out, once for all, the finger-pointing routine: "If only she would submit to me as the Lord commands her to, I'd love her"; or, "If only he would love me, I'd be glad to submit." Our responsibility is non-transferable; there is no contingent feature. "If only . . ." doesn't carry any weight with the Lord. The true motive for right responses from both husbands and wives should be "out of reverence for Christ."

There's More

You may be saying, "I've had enough," but there's more in this text if you're willing to explore it. It goes on to say: A husband should love his wife as his own body, because they are ONE, just as Christians are one with Christ in his body, the church. This means that whatever we do toward our wives we are also doing to ourselves. That explains why you hurt, too, when you're unloving toward her.

Marriage, like our relationship to Christ, has an air of mystery or intrigue about it because it is a lifetime adventure of exploring the mystery of personality in a love relationship toward another.

I Love a Mystery

The concluding verses of this passage demand a close and careful look to gain its full import. I have made a rather free translation to draw out some of the meaning which doesn't come through well in our standard translations: "THIS MYSTERY IS GREAT—and I am speaking with regard to Christ and the church, and in addition to that, YOU (in the marriage relationship), each in his own sphere of responsibility—let each man love his own wife as himself, and each woman fear her husband."

A "mystery" in the New Testament is always a revealed secret, but the information is available only to those who are taught of God. So it is used here, since Paul's main theme in this letter is the truth about the church, and only Christ's own have any real conception of the relationship of Christ to his church. But, though much has been revealed, there is still an element of mystery about our life in the Lord, by God's design. Unlike men, God is never boring or trite; he always has a built-in intrigue factor since he is infinite, eternal, and never lacking in imagination. This is what Paul is using to conclude his teaching on marriage.

One of the joys God has given us is to explore the mystery of personality, both in relation to him and to each other. Have you ever noticed that we never tire of learning about the Lord? He is a tremendously interesting Person! The more we know him, the more we want to know him, in ever-increasing depth of understanding and enjoyment. I'm convinced even eternity will not be long enough to explore fully and know the beauty of his person and character. He is an intriguing personality.

Even so with human personality. It always fascinates me to explore the mystery of God-given human personality. People are tremendously interesting. As with snowflakes, God has made no carbon copies; every single individual is a hand-made original expressing the Creator's uniquely creative touch. I always enjoy standing before a group of people, scanning their faces as I teach, and observe that no two are alike. By contrast, what a drab world it would be if we were all alike. Wouldn't you hate to see a bunch of carbon copies of *you* running around? For my part, one of me is enough— sometimes too much!

Now put this idea into the framework of marriage and what a joy it becomes! Marriage becomes a lifetime adventure of exploring another human personality in a love relationship. This mystery is great! That's the idea Paul wants to leave with us. What a difference it would make if we always viewed it that way. All of us who are married have experienced something of the glory of this truth in the days of courtship and early marriage. Unfortunately, for many "the honeymoon is over." But God never intended it to be so, and it need not be so in *any* Christian marriage.

The Last Word

The final word in our Scripture is instructive: "Let each man love his own wife as himself." Could there be any possibility of marriage failure if we husbands really did this? And to the wives: ". . . let each woman fear her husband." Most English versions soften the impact of this by translating the verb as "reverence" or "respect," but the essential meaning of the Greek text is "fear." It's the word *phobeo* from which we get our English word "phobia." So let's take it straight and see how it fits the context. Can you see, having studied through the passage, why a wife should "fear" her husband?

First, we should clarify the fact that "fear" is used in the same way here that we are to "fear the Lord." We don't grovel in abject terror before him because we know he loves us and has our best interests at heart, but neither do we treat him casually as if he didn't matter. To fear the Lord, as I understand it, is to take him seriously, to care more about what he thinks than about what anyone else thinks or says. I "fear" the Lord as I "fear" electricity. One time I took a 440 volt electrical jolt across my hand and ever since I've had a profound respect for its potential power. Even so with God; I've learned he is not to be taken for granted or treated casually.

Wives, can you fear your husbands in this way? If you desire to please the Lord, you must, for that's what God wants. It's apparent from Ephesians 5 that the husband is God's appointed delegate to assume the responsibility of headship in the marriage and family relationships. This is no joke; it is no easy assignment. This final appeal is to enlist the serious acceptance of this responsibility on the part of the husband and the whole-hearted cooperation of the wife with God's appointed order. When a wife really sees this truth, her heart goes out to her husband to be the kind of helper who will really support him in fulfilling such a demanding assignment.

Again, you will notice that in Ephesians 5:33 there is no mutual contingency clause. We are individually accountable to our Lord to fulfill the function he has assigned—no matter what the response of our mate might be. This means each partner must learn to walk in dependence on His resources through His indwelling life.

Marriage—An Exalted State

In all of this we see that every marriage is designed to be a living portrayal of the union of Christ and his church. Every Christian couple has the high privilege and responsibility of displaying the beauty and glory of this living relationship of a shared life and love. Since God has placed marriage in such a high place, can we do any less? And if there were ever a need for the world to see a Love Story acted out in real life, it's today. But we need to show them the real thing—no fake, no shoddy imitation of human origin. It must be the "love of God which is flooded into our hearts by the Holy Spirit" (Rom. 5:5), as he teaches us to love as Christ loves.

What Love Is Like

God gives us several descriptions of love in his Word. One is in 1 Corinthians 13, which may be helpful to review at this point:

LOVE Described

- PATIENT: long-suffering, the way God is toward us.
- KIND: easy to take, not harsh, e.g., "My yoke is easy . . ." (Matt. 11:30).
- Not ENVIOUS: not wanting everything for itself.
- Not BOASTFUL: not a wind-bag, not vaunting its own worth.
- Not ARROGANT: not inflated with its own importance.
- Not RUDE: rather having good manners, courteous.
- Not SELF-SEEKING: not demanding to have its own way.

- Not TOUCHY: not given to violent reactions on slight provocation.
- Not RESENTFUL: doesn't keep a log book on real or fancied wrongs.
- Doesn't GLOAT over another's sins or misfortunes.
- Is GLAD WHEN TRUTH PREVAILS, even when it hits home.

Another Look at Love

Romans 12 contains another enlightening description of love, especially viewed from the Greek text. Here it is in a literal translation in modern idiom. It starts with a banner headline:

Love—The Real Thing—No Fake

There is no verb in the original language. This grammatical device dramatically focuses the attention on the description of *what love is like* that follows:

LOVE, the kind that puts on no false front: turning away in abhorrence from that which inflicts misery, firmly adhering to that which is beneficial; in brotherly affection warmly loving to one another, leading the way in acknowledging the value in others, not slow to move to action, warm in spirit, having a servant attitude in the Lord, rejoicing in confident expectancy, "hanging in there" under pressure, giving constant attention to prayer, consistently sharing to meet the needs of God's people, earnestly seeking opportunity to be generous to strangers (Rom. 12:9–13).

It's significant to note that this description of love is a running series of participles, with no main verb, thus heightening the descriptive force of the verb forms. Also, the participles are all in the present continuous tense, thus depicting what is to be *a life style* rather than an occasional display of these traits.

There follows, in the balance of Romans 12, a series of present imperatives—demands on the will of the hearer, which constitute *a call to action* in consistent compliance with those demands:

- BLESS your persecutors; DON'T CURSE them!
- DON'T BECOME WISE in your own eyes!
- GIVE to God the maintaining of the right, not avenging yourselves!
- FEED your enemy; GIVE him DRINK!
- STOP BEING CONQUERED by evil;
- CONQUER evil with good!

(Commands in Rom. 12:13–21)

It reads like this then:

Bless the ones persecuting you—bless and stop cursing them: to rejoice with rejoicing ones, to cry with the crying ones, being impartial in your thinking toward one another, not giving your attention to proud and lofty things, but allowing yourselves to be related with those of humble estate. Don't become wise in your own eyes: giving back evil for evil to no one, applying yourselves to that which is morally excellent before all men. Not taking justice into your own hands, beloved, but give room for the wrath (of God), for it stands on record: "setting things right is my prerogative; I will give back that which is due" says the Lord. But if your enemy is hungry, feed him; if he is thirsty, give drink to him; for doing this you will heap coals of fire on his head. (Apparently, that he might become ashamed of his own conduct in the light of your kindness.) Stop being conquered by harmful things, but rather *you* conquer the evil with the good (Rom. 12:14–21, a literal rendering).

To summarize, in slightly different terms:

LOVE—THE REAL THING—NO FAKE

LOVE'S ATTITUDE is:
Discerning, genuinely considerate, ready to act, available, warmly alive, subject to the Lord, joyfully optimistic, persevering, dependent, generous, and actively hospitable (Rom. 12:9–13).

LOVE'S ACTIONS are:
Sympathetic, understanding, compassionate, impartial, humble, not vengeful, easy to live with, even kind to enemies, unconquerable (Rom. 12:14–21).

All these traits are derived from the description of the unfeigned love in the text. What a highly desirable quality of life this is—obtainable by everyone who knows the God whose name is Love.

5.

God's Ideal

To put marriage in true perspective, we need to fill in the background of the relationship as it was first instituted by God and endeavor to see it as he sees it. To do this, let's review Genesis 2:18–25, where we see the beginning of marriage:

GOD'S THOUGHT: Then the Lord God said, "It is not good that the man should be alone; I will make him a helper fit for him."

GOD'S ACTION: So out of the ground the Lord God formed every beast of the field and every bird of the air, and brought them to the man to see what he would call them; and whatever the man called every living creature, that was its name. The man gave names to all cattle, and to the birds of the air, and to every beast of the field; but for the man there was not found a helper fit for him. So the Lord God caused a deep sleep to fall upon the man, and while he slept took one of his ribs and closed up its place

with flesh; and the rib which the Lord
God had taken from the man he made
into a woman and brought her to the
man.

ADAM'S REACTION: Then the man said, "This at last is
bone of my bones and flesh of my flesh;
she shall be called Woman, because she
was taken out of Man." Therefore a
man leaves his father and his mother
and cleaves to his wife, and they become one flesh. And the man and his
wife were both naked, and were not
ashamed.

The Original Model

The central idea in marriage is *oneness,* as seen in Adam's
exulting declaration, "This at last is bone of my bones and
flesh of my flesh . . ." (Gen. 2:23), and, "Therefore . . .
the two shall become one flesh" (Gen. 2:24). This latter
statement is the most frequently repeated word about marriage in the Bible, occurring at least seven times: in Genesis
2:24, Matthew 19:5,6, Mark 10:8 (twice), 1 Corinthians
6:16 and Ephesians 5:31. This emphasis points up the focus
of God's thought on marriage. In the beginning Eve was
taken from Adam, then given back to him—to become one
with him again. Thus each marriage is designed to picture
a restoration of that kind of oneness—a oneness of *person-
hood*: of body, soul and spirit—not just of body. In the phrase
"they become one flesh," the Hebrew word translated "flesh"
can mean "person" as well as "body" or "flesh." That two
shall become *one person* is the predominant idea in marriage. Also, marriage in the Hebrew view was considered a

continuation of God's activity in creation and represented
the blending of two lives in the service of their God in response to his divine call in their joint commitment to him.

God's "Plan View" of Marriage

With this basic idea in mind, let's consider God's *intent*,
his *process*, and his *design* for marriage. For the sake of
brevity and clarity we have put this in outline form:

GOD'S "PLAN VIEW" OF MARRIAGE, Genesis 2:18–25

An outline of the basic, essential features of a marriage relationship.

GOD'S INTENT (Gen. 2:18–20).

• "It is not good that the man should be alone . . ." (Gen.
2:18*a*).
   Here it is apparent that God intended A SHARED LIFE.
   And marriage is in God's plan for man's good!
      *Man was not complete without a partner.
      *Woman was made to be MAN'S COMPANION.
      (For the single person: This does not mean that fulfill-
      ment is not possible without marriage. Though mar-
      riage is the usual provision, companionship is available
      through other means, and the abundant life Christ of-
      fers is available to anyone—married or single.)

• ". . . I will make him a helper fit for him" (Gen. 2:18*b*).
   Here we see a God-APPOINTED ORDER
      She was made for *him*;
      He needs *her*, as a helper;
      *She is suited to his needs—she *complements* him;

*Man and woman are *to work together* in the building of a home and a life;
*They form a *team*—with mutual concerns and responsibilities.

• "The man gave names to the animals . . . but for the man there was not found a helper fit for him" (Gen. 2:20):
  God intended that man should find a SUITABLE PARTNER. Woman was to be quite different from the animals:
  • Not just a beast of burden,
  • Not merely a biological laboratory to bear children,
  • Not a THING to be used and disposed of.

GOD'S PROCESS (Gen. 2:21–22).

• "So the Lord God caused a deep sleep to fall upon the man . . ." (Gen. 2:21).
  The man's unconscious state implies that the marriage relationship is far deeper than surface affection—not just a part of man's conscious life, but reaching into the subconscious.

• "And the rib . . . taken from the man he made into woman" (Gen. 2:22).
  *She is *part* of him, yet *separate* from him.
  *She should be as dear to him and as important to him as his own body.
  *A new relationship is established—a LOVE RELATIONSHIP, since she was made from his side, from a place near his heart.

GOD'S DESIGN FOR MARRIAGE (Gen. 2:23–25)

• Identification—in Life and Destiny.

his at last is bone of my bones and flesh of my flesh" (Gen. 2:23).

". . . and they become one flesh" (Gen. 2:24).

Here we see a *blending of lives* to the exclusion of strictly personal, selfish interests.

> *No longer MY interests, but OUR interests.
> *No longer a union of two bodies, but the union of two lives—body, soul and spirit.

• ". . . she was taken out of man" (Gen. 2:23).

Man's *headship* is implicit here.

• ". . . a man leaves his father and mother" (Gen. 2:24).

All other human relationships are secondary to the marriage relationship. In-laws are OUT, as far as the marriage is concerned; they take second place to the new relationship.

• ". . . a man leaves . . . and cleaves to his wife" (Gen. 2:24b).

This declares that marriage is *permanent—he shall stick to his wife.* Whatever happens, the man should say, "I'm with you."

• "And the man and his wife were both naked, and were not ashamed" (Gen. 2:25).

Nothing to hide from each other, enjoying an open, transparent relationship, fully at ease with each other and with God.

I think we can agree that God's plan is wholly desirable. Why, then, do we find it so difficult to fulfill God's ideal?

Enter "Sin"

Chapter 3 of Genesis, coming right on the heels of what we have just reviewed, describes the disruption of this idyllic scene—as sin enters the picture. And sin always represents a failure on the part of man to achieve the ideal. This fact of life explains why we find it so difficult to attain to God's ideal, whether in marriage or any other relationship. But in spite of the problems imposed by sin God never surrenders the ideal! The whole of biblical revelation is the story of God's redemptive activity to recover man from the clutches of this insidious force.

Love Locked Out . . .

The essence of sin is my insisting on having my own way in opposition to God's way. So the problem in some marriages is that men and women will not draw on the redemptive, healing ministry God has made available to them in Christ—*so they want out!* This brings into focus the matter of divorce—a severance of the marriage relationship. On several occasions our Lord Jesus was faced with the question of why God allowed divorce. One of these is recorded in Matthew's gospel:

> And Pharisees came up to him and tested him by asking, "Is it lawful to divorce one's wife for any cause?" He answered, "Have you not read that he who made them from the beginning made them male and female, and said, 'For this reason a man shall leave his father and mother and be joined to his wife, and the two shall become one'? So they are no longer two but one. What therefore God has joined together, let no man put asunder." They said to him, "Why then did Moses command one to give a certificate of divorce, and to put her away?" He said to them, "For your hardness of heart Moses allowed you to divorce your wives, but from the beginning it was not so" (Matt. 19:3–8).

Note two things about this discourse:
(1) The oneness of marriage is designed to be permanent

—"What therefore God has joined together let no man put asunder."

(2) Divorce was allowed because of the *hardness of heart* in man—his failure to live up to the ideal God has in mind: "For your hardness of heart Moses allowed you to divorce your wives, but from the beginning it was not so." In other words, divorce was an accommodation brought about because of man's sin. Divorce was a second-best arrangement allowed by God to make the best of a bad situation, because men insist on going their *own* way instead of his.

I Hate Divorce

However, there's no doubt about how God feels in regard to divorce. He says it loud and clear:

"For I hate divorce, says the Lord. . . . So take heed to yourselves and do not be faithless" (Mal. 2:16).

Note again, the problem is faithlessness—failing to believe that God can give grace to work out the problems in marriage, resulting in infidelity to the marriage contract.

So we can see that divorce is not part of God's ideal but a *departure* from it. His ideal is one man for one woman for one lifetime. But God has allowed divorce to make the best of a bad situation because of the stony hardness of men's hearts.

"But it was not so in the beginning."

6.

The Divorce Question

If there was ever a difficult and highly controversial question relating to the Word of God, it is the question of divorce. In some ways it is really sticking one's neck out even to attempt to clarify the issues. But there is a crying need for clear understanding and guidelines on this subject. In these days of easy divorces and multiple marriages, with all the pain and complications they bring, there are hurting hearts all around us who need to be helped to an understanding of the heart of God and the healing he desires to impart. So let's try to sort out the pieces on the subject of divorce by facing some obvious questions and seeking biblical answers.

What Is Divorce?

First, we need to decide what divorce is so that we can at least agree on what we're talking about. In doing this we need to look for a practical, life-related definition, not just a technical, legal one that might apply in a court of law. As I understand it, divorce is an official, legal severance of the marriage union designed to free the marriage partners—to terminate one marriage relationship with the possibility in mind of assuming another. Thus, divorce (in man's intent

at least) carries with it the desire and/or right to remarry.
If this were not so, there would be very little point in going
to the trouble of the legal action of obtaining a certificate
of divorce (as mentioned in Matt. 19:7). The question of re-
marriage is always closely linked with the divorce question,
so it seems to me the two questions need to be dealt with
simultaneously as part of the same issue.

Why Divorce?

Since God hates it, why does he allow it?
We could ask the same question about sin of any kind.
Since God hates sin, why does he allow it? The answer to
both questions is: *because of the hardness of men's hearts.*
Since God gave man the power to make uncoerced moral
choices, he has faced himself with the necessity of accepting
man's "Drop dead, God" attitudes. But that doesn't deter
him from moving toward men with the redemptive solutions
designed to win their hearts to obedience to the truth and
the resulting liberty. Thank God that it is so, or we'd *all* be
lost! God hates sin but loves sinners. He also hates divorce
but loves divorcees!

When Divorce?

Let's take the example the Lord Jesus cites in Matthew
19 and see if we think there are any legitimate grounds for
divorce—and if so, why?

And I say to you: whoever divorces his wife *except for unchastity,* and marries another commits adultery (Matt.
19:9).

The phrase "except for unchastity" I take to be a clear-
cut exception our Lord is making to the general rule. From

this we gather that sexual infidelity is legitimate ground for divorce. The reason for this seems clear from the "oneness" idea which our Lord is careful to cite in the context (Matt. 19:5–6). A third party to the marriage union violates the basic oneness of God's ideal. God never said, "The three (or more) shall become one," but rather "The *two* shall become one."

I know there are other interpretive opinions on this passage: the Jewish cultural considerations that this may be talking about unfaithfulness during engagement; the fact that the word for fornication, not adultery, is used (unchastity in the r.s.v.), etc. But the context of the Pharisees' question, "Is it lawful to divorce one's wife for any cause?" (Matt. 19:3); the citing of "a certificate of divorce" (Matt. 19:7); and the seriousness of the matter under consideration lead me to think that our Lord would not leave a matter so important to the uncertainties of merely cultural or verbal consideration. I believe he would speak truth to be clearly understood *by* all generations, *for* all generations, unobscured by Hebrew cultural or Greek language considerations.

I know, too, that in similar passages in the other Gospels our Lord omits the phrase "except for unchastity." But to insist that he must say everything exactly the same way each time is unreasonable and unwarranted. We don't insist on this with each other. And to insist that the Gospel writers record everything in exactly the same way is equally unreasonable. And so that we don't think this is the only time our Lord mentioned this exception, it's good to note that he says essentially the same thing in Matthew 5 in a quite different context:

> It was also said, "Whoever divorces his wife, let him give her a certificate of divorce," but I say to you that everyone who divorces his wife *except on the ground of unchastity,*

makes her an adultress; and whoever marries a divorced woman commits adultery" (Matt. 5:31–32).

The context here is the Sermon on the Mount in which our Lord makes a series of contrasts using the words, "You have heard that it was said . . ." as citing the Mosaic law; and "But I say to you . . ." citing the deeper *intent* and *spiritual content* of God's laws. Thus, when he says ". . . except on the ground of unchastity," he is resting not in legal, Mosaic authority but on *his own authority*. Consequently, we have, not legalistic nitpicking as the Pharisees were inclined to do, but the spiritual intent of the matter declared by the Son of God.

The choice of the Greek *porneia* (translated "unchastity") in both of these passages in Matthew has clear import which aids our understanding of the matter, as well. This word is usually translated "fornication" and pictures prostitution of the marriage relationship—selling out God's ideal for a cheap imitation of what marriage is intended to be. Marriage is more than the joining of two bodies; it is the joining of two lives in a mutual commitment of love just as Christ has joined us to himself by our mutual commitment of love. Any other arrangement "sells out" God's plan for a shoddy substitute.

So we conclude that fornication, or infidelity, is legitimate cause for divorce because it breaks the marriage bond.

Overcoming Grace

Let us hasten to add, however, that merely because one has the biblical grounds for divorce doesn't mean he must seek a divorce. The highest Christian right is being willing to forego one's rights, even as our Lord has done in his coming to be our Savior. And the grace of God manifested in a life can always supersede our personal insistence on the exercise of our rights. As someone has wisely said, "If we insisted on *all* our rights, we'd be in hell."

The Unforgivable Sin?

Speaking of grace: Is not the grace of God available to provide forgiveness in this area of divorce as well as in other realms? I say yes! But somehow, in many quarters, Christians make divorce the unforgivable sin. When God forgives, he *forgets* our sin. Even when *we* remember it, he says, "What sin?" But not so with us in our Pharisaical attitude toward divorcees. We don't even bother to ask them the circumstances of their supposed failure. We just automatically exclude them from areas of Christian service and make them second-class citizens. How many have been wronged this way in the name of Christ!

Guilt and Grace—Some Overriding Principles

If there is any one thing we should be able to say about Christians, it is that we should be *free from guilt*. If we're not, we're missing the whole point and value of the cross of Christ. This should be true of Christians who are divorcees as well as those who are not. Divorce is *not* the unforgivable sin. And what God has forgiven and forgotten we have no business bringing up again. As our dear Dutch evangelist friend, Corrie ten Boom, says, "God has buried our sins in the depths of the sea and put up a sign: 'NO FISHING!'" My wife adds a footnote to this and says, "That's true, but some of us go out and buy deep-sea-diving outfits."

This leads us to seek to set down some background principles to act as guidelines for assessing divorce problems. Here are some I've arrived at:

Guideline Principles on Marriage and Divorce

1. Fulfillment of God's ideal for marriage is always the number one aim.

2. God's ideal is one man for one woman for one lifetime.

3. The Lord is a totally redemptive person, always seeking to make a bad scene into a good one.

4. The overcoming grace of God is always available to restore, reinstate, and surmount the obstacles in response to repentance and faith.

5. Divorce—even wrongful divorce—can be forgiven through Christ's gracious and redemptive provision in the Cross.

6. Forgiveness restores the relationship, but it may not change the situation we have brought on ourselves by our sin. We need to be willing to accept the inevitable consequences of wrong acts, but at the same time be free from guilt.

Problems of Application

Perhaps the most practical way to bring out further truth on this difficult subject is to view some practical examples and the biblical principles which apply.

First of all let's follow through on the case our Lord mentions in Matthew 19 in which one party is guilty of sexual infidelity. In another place our Lord has said, "Out of the heart come evil thoughts, murder, adultery, fornication . . ." (Matt. 15:19). So we see that fornication is the act preceded by the thought. The real problem is a philandering, unfaithful *heart.* This is the basic betrayal of both the marriage vows and the very *intent* of marriage. The unfaithful party says, "I want out." So we have here a "guilty" party and an "innocent" or "wronged" party. The "guilty" party was guilty of violating the oneness of the marriage bond in his or her heart and by overt action. The "wronged" party, though not totally innocent of any wrong, was not guilty of breaking the marriage bond. So, perhaps we can begin to see the reason for our Lord's exception clause: to minimize the damage caused by the "hardness of men's hearts" by not penalizing the "wronged" party for the sin of an unfaithful partner and to free the "wronged" party from the anomaly of a three-party marriage. We reason, then, that God allowed divorce as a kindness to the offended party even though his desire would be the fulfillment of his ideal.

On the basis of this reasoning, the offended party should be free to remarry, free from guilt, free from public censure. After all, he or she may have done everything possible to make the marriage work, and God may have no sin to lay to his or her charge as far as the perpetuation of the marriage is concerned. The offended party may have been wholly unable to forestall the breakup of the marriage because of the philandering heart of the guilty one. After all, in his own love extended to the human race God himself has so arranged it that all unyielding, rebellious men who reject his love will spend an eternity in hell even though he has done all he can to keep them from such a fate.

So we assume that the wronged party in this case is set free from the marriage, by means of divorce—*without penalty.*

But suppose this party finds it possible, through God's grace, to forgive the erring mate and stay in the marriage? It's entirely possible that the unfaithful mate may be won back to repentance by such a display of Christian love and grace. In that case, though the marriage bond has been broken by infidelity, certainly the Lord can reconstitute the marriage, but only if the adulterous relationship with the third party is terminated. At this point I must say that the most beautiful display of the overcoming grace of God I have seen is in wives who have counted on the Lord to redeem their marriage and restore a sinning husband. The principles here are clear: Our redemptive Lord wants to enlist our cooperation to "shape up" the marriage—not to "ship out," even in the face of such obvious and devastating provocation. And we should never minimize the seriousness of the provocation: Unfaithfulness is like a stab in the heart to a faithful mate.

To Review:

1. Is the innocent partner free to seek a divorce if his or her mate is unfaithful? Yes, in accord with Matthew 19:9, the exception clause.

2. Is divorce mandatory when infidelity is involved? No. The grace of God *can* overcome the hurt and win back the erring partner.

3. Can God forgive the sin of infidelity? Yes. See John 8:1–11.

4. If he can, cannot men forgive and restore a right relationship? Yes, through the power of an indwelling Christ whose very nature is to forgive.

5. But doesn't adultery permanently destroy the marriage union? Not if both parties are willing to renew their commitment and seek a better foundation for their marriage— the foundation God has laid in his Word.

6. Suppose the marriage doesn't go together again. Is the guilty party free to remarry? The answer to this would depend on other factors: Did this party become a Christian since the divorce? If so, he should seek to reconcile with his former mate. If that is not possible (perhaps the former

mate has remarried), then he is free to remarry but *only in the Lord* and on the basis of the fact that he is a new creation in Christ (2 Cor. 5:17). I base these conclusions on the principle that God wants to redeem the first marriage if it is at all possible, but he is not interested in penalizing us for sins committed before we came to Christ. In all of this it is assumed that responsibilities incurred through the marriage (like children and their care) are faithfully and willingly fulfilled as part of the inevitable consequences of sin—even though the sin has been forgiven.

7. What if the guilty party is not a Christian and does not become one? In that case he is not free at all—whatever he does—and may proceed to heap sin upon sin, problem upon problem, marriage upon marriage, hurt upon hurt. The only hope for him is to know the forgiveness and life-changing grace available only through knowing Jesus as Lord. Our Christian responsibility toward him is to seek to help him know our Lord Jesus.

8. What about two Christians who have not heeded God's word and are divorced? 1 Corinthians 7:10–11 is a direct answer to this question: Let them remain single or else be reconciled (no time limit specified).

9. How about desertion as a ground for divorce? 1 Corinthians 7:15, I believe, is the answer: If the unbelieving partner desires to depart, let it be so. In such a case the believer is not bound. Two corollary thoughts apply to this: (1) the believer is not to push for termination of the marriage or make it so hot that the unbeliever wants out; (2) desertion by a non-Christian mate has at least the implicit suggestion of infidelity which either has or will take place. So I personally relate this teaching of Paul's closely with the words of our Lord in Matthew 5 and 19, even though Paul is adding some further instruction, as he clearly states in 1 Corinthians 7:12a.

10. Are both infidelity and desertion legitimate grounds
for divorce? I believe so. Fornication, as in Matthew 5:32
and 19:9 is clearly so; and desertion, as in 1 Corinthians 7:15,
with the implicit infidelity that I have suggested as its normal
complement, I believe is equally valid.

11. Are there other grounds for divorce which are legitimate? I see no others in the Scriptures. We sometimes look
for others, such as the welfare of the children or relief from
the emotional stress or physical abuse, but it seems the Lord
really expects us to trust him for all these circumstances as
painful as they may be. However, there are other corrective
means short of the finality a divorce represents. A redemptive
separation may be indicated to shake up the erring partner.
But it must be with truly redemptive motives and with the
door left wide open for reconciliation.

12. Why does God hate divorce? Because it is the painful
rending of a relationship designed to be permanent and because it ruins the picture that marriage is designed to portray
—the beauty of a love relationship between God and man.

There are many more specific conditions which must be
examined in reviewing divorce cases with the desire to help,
and the only thing I know to do is to examine each situation,
and with the specific conditions clearly in mind, to apply the
principles we have reviewed.

We need to ask questions like:

Are both of you Christians? Or just one? Which one?

Do you really want to make your marriage work?

Are you willing to hear what God has to say, and build
a new foundation for your marriage?

Were you both Christians before you divorced? Is there
possibility of reconciliation?

Have you been unfaithful to your marriage partner?
Have you sought forgiveness for this sin?

Are you willing to break off your adulterous relationship?

Are you free from all guilt resulting from your own failures?

Do you believe Christ is able to redeem your situation?

Do you think that divorce is really an answer, or would a changed heart be a better way to go?

Are you willing to take the hurt and trust the Lord to reconstruct and redeem your life situation in spite of all the obstacles you see?

Are you really allowing Jesus to be Lord in you?

In this process we must be taught of God on the scriptural principles to apply. This means doing our homework on some of the basic passages on marriage. Study Genesis 1:27–28, 2:18–25, 3:16–21 in the Old Testament and Matthew 5:1–32; 19:3–12; Mark 10:2–12; Luke 16:18; 1 Corinthians 6:16, 7:1–40; 2 Corinthians 6:14–18; Ephesians 5:21–33; Colossians 3:18–20 and 1 Peter 3:1–7 in the light of the context, and 1 Peter 2:18–25. There's no substitute for your own personal study and investigation of God's Word on this subject; expect to be taught by the Spirit of God.

7.

The Pattern of Fidelity

For Men—The Message of Hosea

God's steadfast love in the face of Israel's infidelity is probably the most pointed illustration of the kind of faithfulness God expects of husbands. The little Book of Hosea in the Old Testament casts Hosea himself in the role of the faithful husband married to a profligate wife. What a story this is, as the pattern of fidelity for men.

This story is so graphically told by Dr. Donald Grey Barnhouse that I have obtained permission to use his exposition of it.

Conquering Love

"What the Christian attitude should be in marriage is illustrated in the greatest and strangest love story in the Bible —that of the prophet Hosea and unfaithful Gomer.

"God said to Hosea, 'I am going to use your life as an object lesson for my people Israel. I command you to marry an immoral woman, and together you will act out a pageant. You will play the part of God, and she will play the part of Israel. Though she will be unfaithful to you, you must love her and be faithful to her, for that is the situation between Me and Israel.' 'So he went and took Gomer the daughter of Diblaim, and she conceived and bore him a son' (Hosea 1:3).

"Hosea and Gomer had three children, and God dictated the name of each, in order to illustrate the tragedy which their willfulness would bring. Of the first child God said, 'Call his name Jezreel,' which means *scattered;* and God has scattered the Jews all over the world.

"Gomer next bore a daughter and God said, 'Call her name Lo-ruhamah,' which means *not pitied*—'for I will no more have pity on the house of Israel, to forgive them at all.'

"Hosea was instructed to name his third child, a son, 'Lo-ammi,' which means *not my people*—'. . . for you are not my people and I am not your God' (Hosea 1:4, 6,9).

"The Book of Hosea is a story of romance, adultery, and enduring love, even the enduring love of God. God says, 'They will live happily ever after,' and he tells Hosea that the names of his children will be changed. The first child will still be called 'Jezreel,' but with the meaning 'God sows' instead of 'God scatters,' for the Oriental sowed seed by throwing it to the ground, with the same motion that he used for throwing something away. 'Lo-ruhamah' becomes 'Ruhamah,' 'pitied'—'. . . for I will have pity on them,' and 'I shall call "Lo-ammi," "Ammi," for they shall be 'my people'" (Hosea 2:22–23). The new meanings illustrate how God's unchanging love covered the multitude of Israel's sins, even as Hosea's love covered Gomer's sins, and therefore how a Christian's love must cover an erring partner's sins.

Gomer and Her Paramours

"Now, Gomer left Hosea and lived with other men; and each lover was poorer than the man before him. One day

Hosea said to a certain man, 'Are you the man who is cur-
rently living with Gomer, the daughter of Dibliam?'

" 'Well, what of it?' replies the man.

" 'I am Hosea, her husband.'

"As the man recoiled, Hosea said, 'But I love her, and I
know that you don't have enough money to take care of her.
Take this money and see that she does not lack for anything.'

"So the man took Hosea's money and bought clothing, oil,
and wine for Gomer, who gave her lover credit for providing
these things; but Hosea said, 'She doesn't know that I paid
the bills.'

"Here is the story as told by God in the words of Scripture: 'Their mother has played the harlot; she that conceived
them has acted shamefully. For she said, "I will go after my
lovers, who give me my bread and my water, my wool and
my flax, my oil and my drink". . . . And she did not know
that it was I who gave her the grain, the wine, and the oil,
and who lavished upon her silver and gold, which they used
for Baal' (Hosea 1:5, 6, 8).

"No doubt the man who took Hosea's money was thinking,
'There is no fool like this old fool.' But who can explain
true love? Love is of God, and it is infinite. Love is sovereign.
Love is apart from reason; love exists for its own reasons.
Love does not operate according to logic but according to
love.

"And we can see Hosea lurking in the shadows to catch a
glimpse of her who fills his heart; weeping as he sees her
embrace her lover and thank him for the gifts which true
love has provided, which villainy offers and folly accepts.

When Man Runs Away

" 'Now,' says God, 'that is how I treat you. You run away
from me and I pay your bills. The story of Hosea is a picture

of my faithfulness. I am the faithful husband and you are the adulterous wife. You turn to other gods; you run away; and still I love you.' Man runs away from God and says, 'I've gotten away from him; I have gotten away from God!' And God touches him on the arm and says, 'My child, I took a shortcut and here I am, to tell you that I love you and am providing for you.' The man pulls away from God and runs; but God says, 'My child, I took another shortcut. I want you for myself.'

"Someone asks, 'Do you mean God loves us even when we run away from him?' Of course he does! Have you never run away from God? And does he not give you the strength to run? God gives a man the breath to say, 'There is no God.' You say, 'Does God love man like that?' God gives man the intelligence to make hammers and nails and axes. God grows a tree and allows man to make a cross from that tree. Then God lets man nail him to the cross. That is how much God loves you. He pursues you because he loves you and wants you to commit yourself to him.

Never-Failing Love

"Thus Hosea kept on loving Gomer, who gradually sank to the depths of degradation. Jehovah announced that this was a picture of his love following unfaithful Israel through the years. 'I will punish her for the feast days of the Baals when she burned incense to them and decked herself with her ring and jewelry, and went after her lovers, and forgot me,' says the Lord. And while his justice allowed her to reap the reward of her deeds, her misery became the framework in which his never-failing love could be exhibited; for of the nation God says, 'I will allure her, and bring her into the wilderness, and speak tenderly to her. And there I will give her her vineyards and make the valley of weeping a door of hope. And there she shall answer as in the days of her youth, as at the time when she came out of the land of Egypt. And in that day, says the Lord, you will call me "My husband," and no longer will you call me "My Baal." And I will betroth you to me forever; I will betroth you to me in righteousness and in justice, in steadfast love, and in mercy. I will betroth you to me in faithfulness; and you shall know the Lord' (Hosea 2:14–17, 19–20).

Gomer on the Slave Block

"Finally Gomer, the wife of Hosea, sank so low that she became a slave; and in accordance with ancient custom in the city of Jerusalem she was put on the slave block, naked. God told Hosea to buy her. Let us visualize the auction in the slave market. Perhaps one man bids ten pieces of silver; Hosea bids eleven. Then the man bids twelve pieces, so Hosea bids thirteen. Finally, the bid is fifteen pieces of silver and a bushel of barley. Hosea bids fifteen pieces of silver and a bushel and a half of barley. The auctioneer intones, 'Sold to Hosea for fifteen pieces of silver and a bushel and a half of barley!'

"So Gomer now belonged to Hosea as a slave. According to the law of that time he could have killed her if he wished. But Hosea tells us what happened: 'The Lord said to me, "Go again, love a woman who is beloved of a paramour and is an adulteress." '

" 'Love her?'

" 'Even as the Lord loves the people of Israel.'

" 'But Lord, she is a harlot, sold on the auction block as an adulterous slave!'

" 'Go love her,' says God, 'love her, even as the Lord loves you.'

God's Faithfulness

"Hosea took Gomer and led her toward their home; and as they went he said to her, 'You must dwell as mine for many days; you shall not play the harlot, or belong to another man; so will I also be to you' (Hosea 3:3).

"The poignancy of Hosea's words grips our heartstrings, for here is the highest expression of love. What Gomer would not voluntarily give him, Hosea now demands because he has redeemed her from slavery. As a purchased slave, she must be faithful. But Hosea's most extraordinary words are, 'So will I also be to you.' In this moment his love shines at its brightest. Although he demands complete faithfulness, he promises to be no less faithful. This is the faithfulness of the love of God. This is the true meaning of the little word 'so' in John 3:16.

"In the light of this story we see the inner meaning of marriage as set forth in the Word of God. Marriage is the union of Christ and the Church.

Married to Christ

"In our salvation we were married to him. He it was who took the vows first of all: 'I Jesus, take thee sinner, to be my Bride. And I do promise and covenant before God and these witnesses, to be thy loving and faithful Savior and Bridegroom; in sickness and in health, in plenty and in want, in joy and in sorrow, in faithfulness and in waywardness, from time for eternity.'

"And then we looked up to him and said, 'I sinner, take Thee, Jesus, to be my Savior and my Lord. And I do promise and covenant before God and these witnesses to be Thy loving and faithful Bride; in sickness and in health, in plenty and in want, in joy and in sorrow, for time and for eternity.'

"Thus we took his name. We were Miss Worldling, but we were married to him and now bear his name, for "Christian" means 'Christ-ian.' When we realize the true meaning of this, we understand how important it is to keep his name spotless before the world.

"I believe that herein is the significance of the Third Commandment which says, 'You shall not take the name of the Lord your God in vain; for the Lord will not hold him guiltless who takes his name in vain' (Exod. 20:7). When a woman takes a man's name, she henceforth honors or dishonors it by every act of her life. We have taken the name of our Lord.

"Christ is the faithful one. We are the ones who slip into flirtation and then into adultery with the world. We are loved by Christ Jesus, but we are drawn aside by our own desires and seduced from our love of Christ. Such a seduction is the worst of all transgressions since it is the sin against the love of Christ. He is faithful to the end, loving us when we were unlovely, and taking us through all steps of our wandering to the place of redemption and final attachment to himself forever.

"Perhaps some believer who reads this may say, 'Lord Jesus, I took you as my Savior but I have been living a worldly life. Just because I gave you sixty minutes and a few dollars on Sunday morning, I thought I was serving you. But I now confess that I have been faithless to you. From now on, Lord Jesus, I will be faithful to you.' To such God replies, 'I will heal their faithlessness; I will love them freely, for my anger has turned from them . . . . They shall return and dwell beneath my shadow, they shall flourish as a garden, they shall blossom as the vine' (Hosea 14:4, 7).

"Perhaps your life partner has been unfaithful and you are asking yourself, 'Have I the love that Hosea had for Gomer? Has my partner seen that I love her that much? Can I really afford such love?' Your old nature will immediately protest, 'No you cannot!' But the Holy Spirit will force you to say, 'Yes, I can!' *

For Women—The Message of Peter

Conquering love is perhaps the major Bible theme, not just for Hosea, but throughout the Scriptures. Peter, in his first letter, has an outstanding presentation of this theme, especially for women.

> Likewise you wives, be submissive to your husbands, so that some, though they do not obey the word, may be won without a word by the behavior of their wives, when they see your reverent and chaste behavior. Let not yours be the outward adorning with braiding of hair, decoration of gold, and wearing robes, but let it be the hidden person of the heart with the imperishable jewel of a gentle and quiet spirit, which in God's sight is very precious (1 Peter 3:1–4).

A study of this passage yields some highly liberating truth. However, to get its real impact we need to retranslate it into somewhat clearer and more accurate form. The Revised Standard Version doesn't really capture the thought very well.

> Likewise, wives, keep on submitting, of your own volition, to your own husbands, in order that if any refuse to be persuaded by the Word they will be won without a word through the life style of their wives, intently observing your manner of life (of wholesome concern to please the Lord) which promotes reverence in them. Of you, let it

---

* Reprinted from "This Man and This Woman" by Donald Grey Barnhouse, by permission of the Evangelical Foundation, Inc., Philadelphia, Pa.

not be the outward cosmetic of braiding your hair and
wearing jewelry, or fashionable dress (on which you depend), but let it be the inner person of the heart, in the
unfading adorning of a gentle and tranquil spirit, which
is of great value before God (1 Peter 3:1–4, a free translation).

Several points are worthy of comment here. Note first that
there is continuing action necessary on the wife's part and
that it is to stem from the willingness of her own heart,
". . . keep on submitting, of your own will." And the husband described is one who simply refuses to hear God's Word
and be persuaded of its truth. He may be, by this description, either Christian or non-Christian.

Next, the verb in verse one reads in some Greek texts,
"*Will* be won," not, "may be won." I believe this to be the
preferred rendering. This achieves the force of a promise, not
just a possibility, and if there's anything a wife needs in this
situation, it's something to cling to from God, instead of a
"maybe" situation. The only thing we must remember in order to balance our thinking is that the timetable is not stipu-
lated. So a wife must trust the Lord for the "when" of the
action as well as the validity of his promise.

But notice this: The whole weight of the wife's confidence
is to be on her own godly life style as the winning weapon.
The man is described as unpersuadable, even by God's Word
—but even beyond the power of the Word is the power of a
life lived in accord with that Word. This is what the wife is
to count on! The display of Christ at work in a yielded
heart is an unbeatable combination. We have in the Greek
passage two ideas which are a bit obscure in our English
translations: (1) that the husband is intently observing his
wife's conduct, and (2) that what he sees excites a reverence
toward God which even the Word did not produce.

This is obviously the inner beauty produced in the wife's life by the Lord who lives in her, and there's nothing more attractive and beautiful to see than the beauty of Christian womanhood. Godly Christian women portray a quality of life which is uniquely theirs; for this, men can only glorify God and give thanks. Would that more women would discover this, instead of going down the dead-end street of Women's Lib! This is not to say that the Women's Liberation movement is all wrong. Some changes are necessary and valid, but they've missed the point of the *best* career a woman can have—that of being a WOMAN.

It's clear, then, that the wife is not to depend on mere outward adorning when she has this far greater potential. This does not mean that she should not seek to be attractive, however. Some women always seem to look like last year's bird's nest, and this is a denial of the very God-given beauty they are meant to display. But in the matter at hand, that of winning a resistant husband, she is to count on the beauty the Lord gives from within, not on what she can paste on the outside. Again, Peter is not arguing against hairdressers, jewelers, and dressmakers, but rather he is putting the emphasis where it belongs—on being a truly Christian person, allowing the indwelling Christ to display the attractiveness of his own life and love. There's a word in verse four which says it: ". . . let it be the *unfading* adorning . . ." The word "unfading" used here is set in contrast with the fading nature of outward cosmetics. Women are always retiring to "repair the damage" as they say, but the inner person of a godly woman is being constantly renewed.

I love the expression, ". . . the imperishable jewel of a gentle and quiet spirit" of the Revised Standard Version in verse four. What a commentary this is on God's design for Christian womanhood! The opposite of this description is the dominant, officious female one sometimes encounters. If there's anything that turns men off, that's it. The strident-voiced, haranguing "fishwife" type is a wholly unattractive version or "perversion" of womanhood. This calls our attention back to the phrase "without a word" in verse one. This is what has been called God's anti-nagging provision. "Without a word," it says. In other words, the wife need not say "one word" to persuade the reluctant male. What he observes is to be so powerful that she has no need to assault his eardrums with a barrage of words. We hasten to add that "without a word" is not initiating a gag rule, or that the wife is to become totally mute, or even to give him the "silent treatment." True submission to her helper role carries with it the responsibility of the wife to confront her husband honestly and lovingly—to help him be the man God wants him to be. But not by nagging! Besides, did you ever recognize that nagging is just a cheap form of verbal blackmail? It says, "Unless you do what I want I'll just wear you out with words." The Lord wants to save us from such basically unavailing approaches.

Why is "a gentle and tranquil spirit" of great value to God? I suppose it's because (1) that's the way the Lord Jesus is, and (2) that's the way women best display the beauty of their womanhood. The Lord Jesus said "I am meek (or gentle)" (Matt. 11:29). Now, meekness is not weakness. It has been described as "power under restraint," or "soft courage." It is a wholly admirable quality, able to take injury without resentment and praise without pride. And a tranquil (or quiet) spirit is, again like the Lord Jesus, the evidence of that trustful confidence in God's care and ability which supplies poise and peace when it seems outwardly that all is lost.

Wives, can you envision what this kind of conduct does to a wayward man? The value of God's way shines like gold, especially when we contrast it with some of the alternatives

—pressuring, manipulating, withdrawing, seducing, nagging, etc.—which are sometimes employed.

But the real punch of this passage in 1 Peter comes in one word—the first word in verse one: "likewise." Whenever we see this word, we should ask, "Like what?" For it is employed to lead us to a comparison. It says, "in the same way"—and we ask, "The same way as what?" The answer is in the context; we need to read what has gone before:

> Servants, be submissive to your masters with all respect, not only to the kind and gentle but also to the overbearing. For one is approved if, mindful of God, he endures pain while suffering unjustly. For what credit is it, if when you do wrong and are beaten for it you take it patiently? But if when you do right and suffer for it you take it patiently, you have God's approval (1 Peter 2:18–20).

If you're like I am, right here you say, "Hold it! Don't you think that's going a bit far?" For normal human responses are not this way. The flesh operates on an essentially "tit-for-tat" basis, so, "If you think I'll sit still and 'take it' when I don't have it coming, you'd better think again!"

Did you ever have the driver in the car behind you lean on his horn just a split second after the light turned green? What was your reaction?

Or did you ever have the boss chew you out for a mistake you didn't make? Most of us manage, in such situations, to put up a pretty heavy barrage of flak to defend our righteous position. But here Peter is addressing a Christian slave and telling him to "take it" even though he had done no wrong! And what he was to take was a literal flogging, not just some verbal abuse.

"But if when you do right and suffer for it you take it patiently, you have God's approval" (1 Peter 2:20*b*). This is supernatural conduct, possible only through the overcoming power of Christ in a life. And what do you suppose was the object of all this pain and strain? Was it not the winning of the overbearing master? Here is *conquering love* at work again.

The Pattern of Christ

And in case we should want some special kind of merit badge for such performance, Peter goes on to explain that this kind of conduct is just normal Christian life. "For to this you have been called, because Christ also suffered for you, leaving you an example, that you should follow in his steps" (1 Peter 2:21).

This behavior is just *normal* for Christians, on four counts:

(1) To this you have been *called,*
(2) Because *this is what Christ did,*
(3) He is your *example,*
(4) You should *follow in his steps.*

"Likewise" in 1 Peter 3:1 is to be (1) like a slave taking an unjust beating graciously, and (2) like Christ, who suffered death for us and took it graciously. Both are actions of love—for the sake of the loved ones.

And in contrast to us, Peter points out that our Lord had *none* of it coming; he took what *we* deserved!

He committed no sin; no guile was found on his lips. When he was reviled, he did not revile in return; when he suffered, he did not threaten; but he trusted to him who judges justly (1 Peter 2:22–23).

The emphasis, I trust, is obvious. We could not say we committed no sin, but he could—that is, he had *no* blame coming. We cannot say no guile was found on *our* lips, but he could. As for reviling, how quick we are to talk back and to respond with threats of retaliation when we are unjustly accused.

The key to Christ's victory (and ours) is in the words, ". . . he trusted to him who judges justly." In essence he said, "It's all right, Father, because I'm counting on you to make it all come out right."

And why did he do all this? Because he loved us, and knew we needed a Savior. For "he himself bore our sins in his body on the tree, that we might die to sin and live to righteousness. By his wounds you have been healed" (1 Peter 2:24). He counted our salvation as more valuable than his own comfort and well-being. He willingly took on himself what we had coming—and thereby won our hearts! "For you were straying like sheep, but have now returned to the Shepherd and Guardian of your souls" (1 Peter 2:25).

He moved to fill our desperate need of a "Good *Shepherd,* who gave his life for the sheep" (speaking of his death *for* us), and a *Guardian,* to direct our lives (speaking of his Lordship and resurrection life *in* us)."

The Ultimate Weapon

"Likewise, you wives," Peter says, "like this example of self-giving love we see in our Lord Jesus . . ." Can you see the validity and potency of this appeal? This is employing God's ultimate weapon, Love! Can you suggest a better way to break down the resistance of an unyielding heart?

Go back and review 1 Peter 3:1–4 now and you'll have the full import of the appeal. And how strong we become, when we draw on this kind of truth! The most beautiful display of Christian·faith I have seen has been wives with hard-hearted husbands, wives who have responded to this word from Peter and "trusted to him who judges justly."

In case you think there's no application of this same truth for husbands, please note that 1 Peter 3:7 says, "Likewise, you husbands . . ." So, for all of us, we have the pattern of Christ—the way of conquering love. Here's the picture in chart form:

LIKEWISE
• *Like a Christian slave,* who acts in love to win his overbearing master, taking a beating when he doesn't have it coming (1 Peter 2:18–20).   • *Like Christ,* who loved us and gave himself for us when he had *nothing* coming to him on his own account—only on our account (1 Peter 2:21–25).

You WIVES (1 Peter 3:1–6)	You HUSBANDS (1 Peter 3:7)
• Be submissive. • Count on what Christ is doing *in you* to win your disobedient mate, (1) not on outward adorning, (2) not on what you say, (3) but on what you *are* in Christ.	• Live considerately with your wife. • Bestow honor on her. • Remember you are joint heirs of the grace of life. • So that your prayers (communication and fellowship with God) may be unhindered.

8.

The Facts
about Fornication

In these days of sexual license and "free love" we need
to take a new look at sex in the light of God's view of marriage. There is a prevalent view that "we can do whatever
we want with our bodies in sexual relations as long as we're
not hurting anyone else." This view totally ignores the teaching of the Word of God about the use and abuse of sex.

First, the Bible tells us that fornication [any sex outside
the God-given function within marriage] is sinning against
one's own body and should be unthinkable if we value our
own well-being: "Shun immorality [fornication]. Every
other sin which a man commits is outside the body; but the
immoral man (fornicator) *sins against his own body*" (1 Cor.
6:18). The implication here is that there are physical or
psychosomatic results of fornication which adversely affect
the body.

Secondly, fornication is sinning against the Lord. In the
same context we read: "The body is not meant for immorality [fornication] but for the Lord, and the Lord for the body"
(1 Cor. 6:13*b*).

Though the thrust of this letter to the Corinthians is to
Christians, I construe this to be the statement of a generality
which includes everyone. That is, the very purpose for which
God gave us bodies is that he might live in these bodies of

ours as his royal residence. So fornication is a violation of God's basic intent in that the fornicator gives his body to the use and gratification of another, not the Lord—in ways that the Lord disapproves.

This argument is further strengthened by the immediate mention of the resurrection: "And God raised the Lord and will also raise us up by his power" (1 Cor. 6:14). This means that even after this life, God lays claim to our bodies. So this is no light matter to be tossed aside as though it didn't count.

The next verses, applied to Christians, move in even closer to the issue: "Do you not know that your bodies are members of Christ? Shall I therefore take the members of Christ and make them members of a prostitute? Never!" (1 Cor. 6:15). It's clear from this that what we do with our bodies involves our Lord in the action. Hence the appeal: Would we seriously, if we thought about it, want to involve the Lord Jesus in prostitution? No wonder the Apostle says, "NEVER!"

The Big Sellout

This leads us to the meaning of the word "fornication," which is itself very revealing. Originally it meant to "sell one's body to indulge another's lust" or to "prostitute one's body for hire." This is "the big sellout" of one's own being for a cheap imitation of the real thing. Today it is not so much the idea of selling one's body for hire, but rather selling out for a momentary satisfaction of the sex drive. The real thing is the fulfillment of sex in marriage. In marriage, sex is designed to be the beautiful physical expression of the commitment of love—the complete union of lives, not just bodies. Fornication is a prostitution of our manhood or womanhood, whether for money or a fleeting moment of sexual gratification.

God is so serious about this that he declares no fornicator shall inherit the kingdom of God:

> . . . walk in love, as Christ loved us and gave himself up for us, a fragrant offering and sacrifice to God. But immorality [fornication] and all impurity or covetousness must not even be named among you, as is fitting among saints. Be sure of this, that no immoral or impure man, or one who is covetous [that is, an idolater] has any inheritance in the kingdom of Christ and of God. Let no one deceive you with empty words, for it is because of these things that the wrath of God comes upon the children of disobedience (Eph. 5:2–3; 5–6).

There is antithesis expressed in this: the kingdom of God (in which Christ is to reign as king in the heart) is set against all the expressions of idolatry, like fornication and covetousness. Idolatry, from the root meaning of the word, is the worship of things which can be seen as opposed to counting of ultimate worth the knowledge of the unseen God. The two are antithetical: One cannot truly count the values of an unseen God as worthwhile if his heart is sold out to coveting or fornicating, and vice-versa.

A similar passage in 1 Corinthians 6:9–10 expands the list to include other forms of idolatry, such as drunkenness, robbery, and homosexuality—but then adds: "And such *were* some of you. But you were washed, you were sanctified, you were justified in the name of the Lord Jesus Christ and in the Spirit of our God."

In other words, God has no place in his kingdom for any of these mentioned, since their hearts are committed to the reign of other things. But he has plenty of room for those who (by making Christ their King) have made these things part of their *past*. His redeeming grace can always overcome the grip of past sins, and making Christ our Lord renders the continuation of these things totally unacceptable, since they are incompatible with our new life in Christ. Continued engagement in these idolatrous sins should cause serious questioning as to the reality of one's Christian commitment.

> For you know what instructions we gave you through the Lord Jesus. For this is the will of God, your sanctification: that you abstain from immorality [fornication]; that each of you know how to take a wife for himself [or better, "possess his vessel"] in holiness and honor, not in the passion of lust like heathens who do not know God; that no man transgress and wrong his brother in this matter, because the Lord is an avenger in all these things, as we solemnly forewarned you. For God has not called us for uncleanness, but in holiness. Therefore whoever disregards this, disregards not man but God, who gives his Holy Spirit to you (1 Thess. 4:2–8).

When Is a Marriage?

With the increasing practice of "just living together" without the formality of marriage, it has become necessary to examine what comprises a true marriage. Is marriage just an old-fashioned, out-dated part of the "establishment" order? Should it be scrapped? Some, especially in the younger generation, honestly think so. We need to examine this matter from biblical, practical, and legal viewpoints.

From the biblical perspective, marriage is viewed as a covenant or agreement, as in Malachi 2:13–16:

> You cover the Lord's altar with tears, with weeping and groaning because he no longer regards the offering or accepts it with favor at your hand. You ask, "Why does he not?" *Because the Lord was witness to the covenant between you and the wife of your youth,* to whom you have

been faithless, though she is your companion and *your wife by covenant.* Has not the one God made one and sustained for us the spirit of life? And what does he desire? Godly offspring. So take heed to yourselves and let none be faithless to the wife of his youth. For I hate divorce, says the Lord God of Israel (Mal. 2:13–16a).

We observe several things from this:

(1) Marriage is a covenant between man and wife, *before God.*

(2) It is God who makes them one.

(3) In doing this he "sustains the spirit of life," that is, there is life-sustaining import to the oneness God imparts. (Apart from this it becomes death . . . not life.)

(4) God's aim is godly children (who are the result of a godly marriage relationship).

(5) God says, "Don't be faithless," and faithlessness is always a departure from an agreement.

So, when is a marriage? In God's sight it's when both parties say "I do" before him, thereby going on record as agreeing to certain stipulations.

What are these stipulations? Well, as far as God's desire is concerned, they are the ones he has given in his Word, as discussed in previous chapters. This is the biblical view of what constitutes a marriage.

As far as the legal aspect is concerned, there are civil marriages and common-law marriages, both designed to deal only with the practical matters surrounding marriage. Usually God is nowhere in view in these "legal" marriages; his truth about the marriage relationship is not invoked.

The question often comes, "I love her so why wait for marriage for sexual intercourse?" But the question needs to be reversed. If you love her, why not wait for marriage? And the only honest reply would be, "Because I don't want to wait," thus proving that you don't really love her enough to commit yourself to her irrevocably in marriage before intercourse.

Then too, we hear, "Why a public wedding?" And though we can understand some reaction to the "wedding extravaganza," it seems we need to reverse the question and ask, "Why, are you ashamed of your partner, or your love relationship?" And, "Don't you want to include your friends in the celebration?"

There are certain practical considerations involved in any public commitment to marriage, whether it is a Christian or civil ceremony:

> The legal protection of any heirs, made firm by the public commitment and documentation.
>
> The security it gives the wife against the man's walking out at his own convenience, without any legal or moral responsibilities.
>
> The confirmation of the couple's understanding of the marriage arrangement, especially of their individual responsibility.
>
> The celebration of a wonderful event with friends and loved ones, to share the joy of their love for each other.
>
> The out-front, glad acknowledgment of each other as marriage partners, instead of being (or seeming) half ashamed to declare their love fully.

(It's clear, I trust, that a Christian wedding gives fuller expression to some of these values than a civil ceremony.)

A Wife Speaks Out about Sex and Marriage

A woman's viewpoint, expressed by Opal Lincoln Gee, says it well:

"I'm for marriage! I've read many prophecies that our social mores will change and have pondered the intensifying
propaganda for so-called sexual freedom. Yet I'm still for marriage. I'm for the *freedom* of marriage. The prospect of
having a dozen different love affairs during my life appalls
me with its restrictions. And I say this after being married to
the same man for nearly twenty-two years.

"We may as well start with sex. Give me the liberty of
the marriage bed. Give me the freedom of a sexual relationship with one lifetime partner. Give me the complete
abandon of the physical and spiritual oneness found only in
married love.

"In marriage there is freedom from fear. How I'd hate to
be hemmed in by the fears I know I'd feel in a transitory
relationship. Improvements in birth control methods have
taken away much of the fear of conception. Still, thousands
of illegitimate babies are born every year. Even in marriage
the possible consequence of the mating act can at times in-
hibit a woman's response to it. Outside marriage, where these
fears are multiplied many times, what freedom could a
woman enjoy?

"There is also freedom from comparison. I am not trou-
bled by a gnawing fear that I might not be living up to a
former partner's performance. There is a satisfying security
in the knowledge that I did not lure my husband from the
embrace of another woman and, because he, too, wholeheartedly believes in marriage, no other woman can alienate him
from me because her body is more seductive.

"There is freedom to grow old within the comfort of my
husband's love. I don't think I could bear the agony of being
discarded when my physical capacities in this realm, as in
others, lose the vigor of youth.

"Marriage has made me a mother four times. I would hate
to be an unmarried mother—and not only because it is still

frowned upon by society. What glorious freedom there is in being able to share the joy of a baby's birth and growth with a husband, who usually feels the same pride and elation in this greatest of all joint enterprises. How fenced in I would have felt had I been required to act modestly with everybody!

"There are countless memories of shared joys and sorrows in a good marriage. I'd hate being cheated of these. There have been hundreds of shared small triumphs and of private jokes that are funny only to us. It takes a while for a man and a woman to build up this kind of easy mental intimacy.

"I am not bored but rather comforted by the knowledge of how my husband will react to almost any situation. I don't have to be tormented with self-doubts when he is quieter than usual; years of living with him have taught me that he is worried about something, not disenchanted with me. I wasn't always sure those first few years.

"In marriage I find freedom to grow as a whole person. I don't think this would be possible for me with any relationship less intimate and binding. Because I don't have to be constantly concerned with my seduction rating, I have energies with which to pursue my interests and nurture whatever talents I have. No doubt this makes me more interesting to my husband. It certainly fulfills a deep need in me.

"I think marriage also enriches my social life. I have more and better friends among both sexes than I could have as a single person. I consider many men my good friends. We have delightful conversations. I don't have to worry about impressing them, and they don't have to be wary of me.

"I suppose monogamy is one kind of freedom and the "new morality" is another, and I grant that the price of marital freedom is high. One has to give up a great deal of selfishness in order to achieve peace and happiness with another person. I would not say that my husband and I were each the one perfect choice for the other. At times, we've felt madly incompatible! Yet the territorial rights and freedom of marriage have given us space to grow, not only as separate beings but in an ever-deepening oneness that has brought us much happiness.

"It has given life to four other happy human beings, too. I can't see how "free love" could ever produce this kind of happiness for people. No doubt it satisfies physical passion. Yet I wonder how much tenderness you would find in a man unwilling to give his name to and sacrifice himself for his possible unborn child? How much real love is there in a woman concerned only with herself, her sex partner, and the thrill of the moment?

"With America's emphasis on sex, it isn't any wonder that even very young people come to believe that sexual gratification is the "pearl of great price," worth the exchange of all other treasures. Unfortunately, by the time many of them find out that other treasures are highly valuable also, it is too late. They have thrown them away on somebody who doesn't know diamonds from rhinestones.

"I believe that the God who made us gave us marriage because He knew it would bring us the highest happiness. Some call this naivete. Others consider it romanticism. To them I can only offer my own experience in reply: Marriage has brought great happiness to me." *

(By Opal Lincoln Gee, Springfield, Mo.)

Some Never Are the Real Thing

Some marriages never are a true marriage in the way God designed marriage should be—whether with or without a wedding ceremony. So a ceremony doesn't make a marriage. A real marriage is a matter of heart commitment to the mar-

---

* Copyright 1968 by *Christianity Today*. Reprinted by permission.

riage covenant. And a whole-hearted commitment can be
made only when both parties understand and agree to the
terms of the agreement. A wedding is the public, forthright
declaration of intent. A Christian wedding is the declaration
of the joint commitment of bride and groom to fulfill God's
design for marriage and to allow him to use their love relationship to show a love-starved world what real love is all
about. Incidentally, in such a Christian wedding, the couple
is making no guarantee to perform perfectly in accord with
their vows, but they are going on record as to their intent and
their willingness to be brought back to their commitment
whenever they fail to keep it. And the one who draws them
back is the gracious third party to every Christian marriage—
the Lord Jesus himself. His design for marriage is great, and
his concern is to help us enjoy all he has planned. It is folly
to settle for less than total fulfillment. We only short-change
ourselves if we do not thoroughly study and wholeheartedly
subscribe to God's plan. Yet, I am constantly amazed at the
number of otherwise knowledgeable Christians who have
never seriously considered the vital information in God's
Word on this subject. We will sign up for courses on wood-
working, knitting, ceramics, Greek mythology, psychology,
wine-making, and ancient history, but it seems there's a con-
spiracy to keep us from majoring in marriage, the most important human relationship we know.

   When is a marriage—really? When there is a blending of
two lives in the beauty of God's design, with Jesus Christ
mediating the full and free exchange of love in a mutual enjoyment of each other and concern for one another. To settle
for anything less is to cheat yourself.

9.

Modern Tragedy
in An Ancient Setting

We observe the tragic breakup of marriages and homes in our day, with its attendant heartache and heartbreak, and wonder at the cause for so great a calamity. An ancient story, from Ezekiel 16, sets forth the answer, I believe, for then and now.

Perhaps you're aware of the fact that God has given us the history of the nation of Israel as a picture of ourselves so that we may learn from it and avoid some of the same folly. Ezekiel gives us a pointed illustration of this fact:

Again the word of the Lord came to me: "Son of man, make known to Jerusalem her abominations, and say, Thus says the Lord God to Jerusalem: Your origin and your birth are of the land of the Canaanites; your father was an Amorite, and your mother a Hittite. And as for your birth, on the day you were born your navel string was not cut, nor were you washed with water to cleanse you, nor rubbed with salt, nor swathed with bands. No eye pitied you, to do any of these things to you out of compassion for you; but you were cast out on the open field, for you were abhorred, on the day that you were born.

"And when I passed by you, and saw you weltering in your blood, I said to you in your blood, 'Live, and grow up like a plant of the field.' And you grew up and became

91

tall and arrived at full maidenhood; your breasts were formed, and your hair had grown; yet you were naked and bare.

"When I passed by you again and looked upon you, behold, you were at the age for love; and I spread my skirt over you, and covered your nakedness: yea, I plighted my troth to you and entered into a covenant with you, says the Lord God, and you became mine. Then I bathed you with water and washed off your blood from you, and anointed you with oil. I clothed you also with embroidered cloth and shod you with leather, I swathed you in fine linen and covered you with silk. And I decked you with ornaments, and put bracelets on your arms, and a chain on your neck. And I put a ring on your nose, and earrings in your ears, and a beautiful crown upon your head. Thus you were decked with gold and silver; and your raiment was of fine linen, and silk, and embroidered cloth; you ate fine flour and honey and oil. You grew exceedingly beautiful, and came to regal estate. And your renown went forth among the nations because of your beauty, for it was perfect through the splendor which I had bestowed upon you, says the Lord God" (Ezek. 16:1–14)

The beauty of this story is the beauty of the greatest love story of all time—*God's love for man.* Ezekiel pictures Israel as a beautiful young girl to whom the Lord plights his troth and with whom he enters into a marriage contract: "When I passed by you again and looked upon you, behold, you were at the age of love; and I spread my skirt over you, and covered your nakedness: yea, I plighted my troth to you and entered into a covenant with you, says the Lord God, and you became mine" (Ezek. 16:8). But the beauty of this picture was soon spoiled:

But you trusted in your beauty, and played the harlot because of your renown, and lavished your harlotries on any passer-by. You took some of your garments and made for yourself gaily decked shrines, and on them played the harlot; the like has never been, nor ever shall be. You also took your fair jewels of my gold and of my silver, which I had given you, and made for yourself images of men, and with them played the harlot; and you took your embroidered garments to cover them, and set my oil and my incense before them. Also my bread which I gave you—I fed you with fine flour and oil and honey—you set before them for a pleasing odor, says the Lord God. And you took your sons and your daughters, whom you had borne to me, and these you sacrificed to them to be devoured. Were your harlotries so small a matter that you slaughtered my children and delivered them up as an offering by fire to them? And in all your abominations and your harlotries you did not remember the days of your youth, when you were naked and bare, weltering in your blood. And after all your wickedness (woe, woe to you! says the Lord God), you built yourself a vaulted chamber, and made yourself a lofty place in every square; at the head of every street you built your lofty place and prostituted your beauty, offering yourself to any passer-by, and multiplying your harlotry" (Ezek. 16:15–25).

There is a modern tragedy acted out in Israel's history. Ezekiel describes it: "You prostituted your beauty, offering yourself to any passer-by . . ." (Ezek. 16:25).

The result is predictable:

"How lovesick is your heart, says the Lord God, seeing you did all these things, the deeds of a brazen harlot; building your vaulted chamber at the head of every street, and making your lofty place in every square. Yet you were not like a harlot, because you scorned hire. Adulterous wife, who receives strangers instead of her husband! Men give gifts to all harlots; but you gave your gifts to all your

lovers, bribing them to come to you from every side for
your harlotries. So you were different from other women
in your harlotries: none solicited you to play the harlot;
and you gave hire, while no hire was give to you; therefore
you were different" (Ezek. 16:30–34).

A lovesick heart—unsatisfied, unfulfilled, frustrated—
mistaking sex for love, is the inevitable result of infidelity,
whether in unfaithfulness to a marriage partner or to God.
Both are portrayed in this unhappy story.

The irony of this course of action is seen in verses 33 and
34:

> "Men give gifts to all harlots; but you gave your gifts
> to all your lovers, bribing them to come to you from every
> side for your harlotries. So you were different from other
> women in your harlotries: none solicited you to play the
> harlot; and you gave hire, while no hire was given to you;
> therefore you were different" (Ezek. 16:33–34).

Men usually pay prostitutes, but here's a harlot who pays!
As with Israel, so with us; there's no way to escape paying
for our folly, whether it is infidelity toward a mate or toward
God.

The next chapter in the story is not a happy one. Israel is
plundered and ravaged by those who were her lovers, as the
inescapable retribution of her outraged husband, God. Here
is one of the most sobering truths in all the Word of God:

> "Because you . . . have enraged me with all these things;
> therefore, behold, *I will requite your deeds upon your
> head,* says the Lord God" (Ezek. 16:43). *"I will deal with
> you as you have done,* who have despised the oath in break-
> ing the covenant . . ." (Ezek. 16:59).

What devastating truth!
But that's not the end.

Steadfast Love . . .

In all the misery of infidelity, can there be a happy ending? Based on the unchanging character of God's love, Ezekiel says "Yes!"

". . . yet I will remember my covenant with you in the days of your youth, and I will establish with you an ever-lasting covenant" (Ezek. 16:60).

"I will establish my covenant with you, and you shall know that I am the Lord, that you may remember and be confounded, and never open your mouth again because of your shame, *when I forgive you all that you have done,* says the Lord God" (Ezek. 16:62–63).

In spite of all the provocation given him by Israel—and by us—God still waits to redeem and bless. Amazing love! This *love that never lets us go.*

Where Is Your Heart?

In light of all you understand of the love of God, can you turn away from him to the fleeting fantasies of things that fade? And in the light of all you know of God's design for marriage, can you turn away from the beauty of his way to the prostitution of your humanity in the emptiness of infidelity?

Where is your heart?

The problem of unfaithfulness in marriage is merely the reflection of a deeper problem—unfaithfulness to God.

God says, "Have a heart! For me—and for your mate!

"Fulfill MY LOVE STORY . . . the real thing."

Epilogue - Happy Endings

We began this "story" with a question: "Where do I begin to tell the story of how great a love can be?" By now I hope you have begun to see the answer and to understand something of the unsearchable depths of the love that is freely available to us in Christ. His love story can be yours; whether worked out in marriage or not, your life can have a happy ending, beginning—and in-between. This is how I've found it:

OUR LOVE . . . and HIS

We love—and somehow seem to feel it all began with us.
The sense of joy and sweet fulfillment fill our hearts
So we forget our style of life was not always thus.
But then we see: the One whose name is Love began it all;
The whole idea is His, in scope and breadth our minds can
 scarce recall.
"Lamb slain before the world began" is how the record sets
 it forth.
Long before our hearts were taught to know the value of
 His worth.

Our love? How frail and fragile it would seem to be—
So soon offended, quick to change—not founded in eternity.
But then He shares His love;
Himself He gives, to live in us.
Now we, frail vessels that we are, receive an inexhaustible
    supply.
Kept in His hands, we have become a well that never will
    run dry.
Great God of grace, we owe to you, at very least, the living
    out of love-filled lives—
And love's response to you, the One in whom our own love
    thrives.
Ours is love indeed—with Yours to fill its deepest need.

The Lord, who loves us so dearly delights to write happy
endings to our otherwise dismal lives, for he is the one who
". . . by his mighty power at work in us is able to do far
more than we would ever dare to ask or even dream of—
infinitely beyond our highest prayers, desires, thoughts, or
hopes" (Eph. 3:20, The Living Bible).